LESSONS IN LEADERSHIP

Making The Move From Manager To Leader

Ben Olson

Copyright © 2014 Ben Olson
All rights reserved. No part of this publication may be reproduced or transmitted in any form or by any means, electronic or mechanical, including photocopy, recording, or any information storage and retrieval system, without the written permission of the author or his assigned agent.

ISBN: 1495963659
ISBN-13: 9781495963650

LESSONS IN LEADERSHIP IS RESPECTFULLY DEDICATED TO:

Shelby Olson
Best friend, true love and my life's Master Gardener

Managers Making the Move
All those who work tirelessly every day to become better Leaders to the teams they serve

CONTENTS

Acknowledgements vii

From the Author ix

Let The Learning Excursion Begin! 1
- o This book is different - and it's just for you
- o Your leadership legacy begins today

Lesson 1: The Fundamentals of Leadership 5
- o Understanding and using the power of perception
- o How to look, think and act like a Leader

Lesson 2: Leaders Are Master Gardeners 12
- o The four truths of our human connection
- o Are Leaders born or are Leaders made?

Lesson 3: Manager vs. Leader: What's the Difference? 22
- o Behaviors that will move you from Manager to Leader
- o A Leader's simple problem solving process

Lesson 4: Key Leadership Behaviors 33
- o The power of self-confidence and a courageous attitude
- o Build your credibility by establishing trust
- o Provide crystal-clear communications
- o Constantly develop the team

Lesson 5: Building Your Team 64
- o Selection, orientation, training and development
- o The *Observe – Question – Plan – Act* approach

The Leader's Tool Box 83
- o   Creating Tactical Action Plans
- o   Preparing your team for the unexpected
- o   Using team incentives vs. individual incentives
- o   Dealing effectively with change begins with a choice
- o   Recommended resources, words of wisdom and more!

ACKNOWLEDGEMENTS

Professional Guidance
The following individuals have provided me with guidance and inspiration during my leadership journey.

Working with each of you has been a privilege.

Aylwin Lewis, Tom Cagle, and Kenny Doiron

Editing and Consultation
Lauren Olson

Trainer-extraordinaire, editor-in-chief, master of detail and awesome daughter.

Special Appreciation
Daughters Melissa and Cara Olson for being a constant source of youthful inspiration and fatherly pride.

Ronnie, Charlie and Josie Krahn for teaching me, through their example, the important life lessons of family values, hard work, hope and courage.

FROM THE AUTHOR

These Lessons Will Put You on the Path to Success!
When I first earned a promotion to a leadership position, I received no training to develop my skills. The unwritten rule seemed to be: *If you received the promotion, you must know what you are doing, so now go do it!* Sound familiar? Unfortunately, I have talked with thousands of newly promoted leaders over the years that have had the same experience.

If you have been thrust into a position of leadership with little or no training, this book contains the lessons you need to jumpstart your new role and get you on the path to become the Leader you want to be. If you are serious about making the move from "Manager to Leader," or if your job is to help others make the move, this book is for you! Your lessons will include:

- Key behaviors that, when utilized, will cause you to be immediately recognized as an effective Leader.
- The power of perception: how to look, think and act like the Leader your team expects you to be.
- The truths of our human connection and how Leaders use these truths to strengthen their team.
- How to build an extraordinary team through selection, orientation, training and development.
- Simple Leader-led processes that will help you to solve problems, create action plans and develop team members.
- Leading through periods of change, preparing for the unexpected, resources for the future and much more!

Every chapter is filled with real life lessons that will cause you to think like a Leader and activities to help you behave like a Leader from day one.

As Zig Ziglar said, *"You can't start the next chapter of your life if you keep re-reading the last one."* It's time to turn the page and begin your Leadership journey today!

LET THE LEARNING EXCURSION BEGIN!

"You can't <u>make</u> people do anything. The most you can hope for is to show them how to do it, and then say, follow me."
Isaac Stern, Master Violinist

Welcome, Leaders! For the next 90 plus pages, I will be your Learning Tour Guide, taking you on an excursion into the wonderful world of leadership. The illustrations and stories contained here detail several of my personal "leadership learning" moments. Most are positive. Others are not. All are real life lessons I have personally experienced. Some people may refer to them as mistakes, but as motivational speaker Cherie Carter Scott once said, "There are no mistakes, only lessons." By applying what you learn in each lesson, you will strengthen your core leadership skills. I know that Leaders are pretty busy people, so you'll find a handy recap page titled "The Leader's Notebook" at the end of each lesson. This page summarizes the key learning points and offers suggestions of developmental actions you can take to sharpen your leadership skills.

This Leadership Book is Written for You
There are hundreds of books about leadership on the market today, and many great ones at that. You can find a list of my personal favorites on the Resource Page for your consideration. The idea for writing <u>Lessons in Leadership</u> came to me after several people mentioned that many leadership books are not relevant to the average small business Leader/operator. They provide illustrations

from the likes of Jack Welsh, former CEO of General Electric. Few can argue the success of Mr. Welsh and his leadership expertise. The problem is that most of us do not operate a multi-billion dollar corporation, have 300,000 employees, or draw a 12 million dollar salary. It can be difficult, if not impossible, to relate to the leadership and organizational challenges that exist at that level. <u>Lessons in Leadership</u> contains illustrations and sound advice that the average Manager, multi-unit Manager or small business owner <u>can</u> relate to. With over 30 years of managerial, supervisory, training and leadership experience in both the retail and food service industries, I have been where you are. I have lived the joys and obstacles of developing and leading a high performing team.

I know the daily grind of the General Manager, and I have experienced the challenges faced by multi-unit Leaders and small business owners. All that said, I must admit I am far from the perfect Leader. I don't claim to have all the answers, nor have I been a perfect model for great leadership behavior, as you will soon see. The value you will find in this book is the sharing of my experiences that will open your eyes to the truths of leadership, and the behaviors Leaders need to display in order to be successful. You will learn as I did, that being a successful Leader is *less* about you and *more* about your team. The degrees to which you nurture, develop, support, love and respect them will tally up to become your leadership legacy.

You Can Begin Building Your Leadership Legacy <u>Today</u>
If you had to leave your current assignment due to a promotion, a transfer or maybe another job all together, how would you like your current staff to remember you?

I once worked as the Training Center Manager for a Fortune 500 food service company. I've estimated that during a five-year period, I trained over 10,000 people for that organization alone.

LET THE LEARNING EXCURSION BEGIN!

One Saturday afternoon, 12 years after leaving that job, I went to a local fast food restaurant to pick up a quick dinner for my family. Standing in line, I could not help noticing the manager, who seemed to be staring at me. When I approached the counter, he said, "Hi, aren't you Ben Olson?" I said yes, and asked how he knew me (because unbeknownst to him at that moment, I honestly had no memory of him). "You were my trainer in orientation class. We played a game about customer service. I won and you gave me a framed picture of Mickey Mouse." The memories came flooding back as I began to recall him and the orientation classes I had taught. "I'm flattered that you remember me after all these years," I said. I'll never forget his response. "Back then I was just a team member, but I worked my way up to General Manager. Believe it or not, I still have that picture of Mickey Mouse. It's hanging in my son's bedroom. Your message of how to provide great customer service really stuck with me." Pointing to a group of award certificates on the wall he exclaimed, "Look, my team has won customer satisfaction awards three years in a row!" I left the building feeling very humbled that I had made such an impression on this young man. I also questioned if I left that same impression with some of the other 9,999 people I trained for the organization.

Here's another, more sobering example, recently shared by an associate of mine.

"Several years ago a man who was my supervisor passed away. He was what I would call a 'quiet Leader'. He never boasted of his accomplishments, although they were many. He often gave of his own time to train and develop members of his team, including me. He was always helpful to everyone – he would be the last one to complain, the first one to offer help, and always without great fanfare. After the funeral, a dinner was hosted by the family for the people he had worked with. Almost immediately the conversation became filled with stories of how this man showed his love and respect for the people on his team. Through his daily actions he quietly built

a legacy of making a positive difference in the lives of everyone he worked with. I remember leaving that dinner feeling even more honored to have known him and wondering out loud what people will be saying of me when my time comes. That experience continues to remind me that being a good Leader is all about helping other people to be their best. If I can accomplish that, everything else related to the success of my business will naturally unfold, as it did for him."

We are seldom aware of all the people we influence every day, let alone during our lifetime. Yet Leaders understand that we do in fact influence – for better or worse – everyone we come in contact with. We build our leadership legacy one day, one action and one person at a time. As you continue reading, I encourage you to think about what you want your leadership legacy to be.

Leadership is a Choice – Your Choice
Isaac Stern was right when he said, *"You can't _make_ people do anything. The most you can hope for is to show them how to do it, and then say, follow me."* No one can _make_ you become a better Leader. Simply reading books or attending seminars won't do the trick, either. As soon as you choose to take actions that will develop your leadership skills, you will be on your way to becoming a better Leader and building your leadership legacy. So your success begins with making that choice. My hope is that you will learn from my experience, lessons and choices. Now, if you are ready to begin your leadership journey, *follow me.*

LESSON 1

THE FUNDAMENTALS OF LEADERSHIP

"People will follow a leader who is strong but wrong before they will follow a leader who is weak but right."

President Bill Clinton

By definition, your role as a Leader begins when people start to follow your direction. Believe me; people yearn to follow Leaders who demonstrate strength, passion, wisdom and clarity. How do they measure you? At first, it's perception. Later, and more importantly, it's what you say and do that will establish your leadership credibility.

What Every Leader Needs to Understand About Perception
Ultimately, it is your "followers" who will observe and determine the quality of your leadership ability. You are measured by your team on your behaviors every day. Managers get defensive about being measured by the team. They believe team members base their opinion of them on "perception" alone, and argue that perceptions are not always accurate. While there is some truth to that argument, Leaders know better. We understand that, right or wrong, people perceive leadership on their own terms. And, in the end, perception – in all its muddied glory – is reality. Like it or not, we have to accept that fact and deal with it.

A Sunday Morning Lesson in Perception
My first learning experience about the role that perception plays in leadership occurred early in my career. It was a Sunday morning and I had just returned home with my family from church services when my boss called. He was out jogging and needed me to meet a construction supervisor at our restaurant. Still in my suit and tie from church, I arrived at the restaurant and met with the construction supervisor about our remodeling plans. Soon my boss arrived, still in his jogging outfit and looking every bit a jogger who worked up a good sweat after running a few miles. Even after introducing himself as my superior, the construction supervisor continued to look at me when asking questions about the project.

Finally, my exasperated boss said, "Excuse me, but you *do* know that I'm in charge of this remodel project, so I'll be making these decisions, right?" To which the construction supervisor replied, "Oh, I'm sorry," and pointing to me in my Sunday suit said, "I just assumed...." Of course what he assumed, or rather what he perceived, was that I was the decision maker because I looked the part. My boss never let me forget this incident, although I did notice he stepped up his wardrobe to look more "supervisory", as he put it.

Fundamental Expectations of the Follower
Beyond perception, followers have certain initial expectations of their Leader. Your team is looking for someone to follow that they can trust and believe in, someone to show them the way. There are a multitude of studies that have basically come to the same conclusion. The most effective Leaders meet or exceed three basic expectations of their followers. Your team expects you to:

THE FUNDAMENTALS OF LEADERSHIP

<u>Look</u> like a Leader

When I was a young cook, I got to thinking that it would be more fun being the boss. I mentioned this to my manager and his response was, "So, you want to be the Leader?" "Yes, sir, that's what I want to do," I replied with excitement. "How do I get started?" I asked. "Well, if you want to be a Leader you need to look like one. For starters, you need to shave every day, cut your hair, polish your shoes and wear a clean, pressed shirt." At the time I was a bit taken aback, but later I was grateful for his candor. The next day I reported to work looking quite different than the day before. Not only did I *feel* differently, but people began to *respond* differently to me as well. My ideas and suggestions began to be taken more seriously. Simply looking the part of a Leader changed people's perception of me, and for the better.

Leaders look the part. Maintaining a neat, clean, "crisp" appearance makes all the difference in how you feel about yourself as well as how others perceive you. Please understand, this concept has little to do with the outward appearance of your body. It's about how you present yourself. For example, my descriptors of maintaining a neat-clean-crisp appearance can be applied to everyone regardless of their weight, height, length of hair, or physical challenges. Do you prefer your hair longer than most? No problem, just make sure it's clean and well-combed.

Are you self-conscious due to your weight, feeling you are too heavy or too thin? Simply wear clothes that fit properly and keep them clean and pressed. Remember that physical imperfections are only that – imperfections. And since no one is perfect, congratulations! You fit right in with the rest of us!

Think like a Leader
Managers focus on short term problem solving. Leaders are more "forward looking", always thinking ahead to build the team and the business and also more focused on their team than themselves.

For example:

Manager	*moves to* ➜	**Leader**
I will do it all		You can do it (Encourage)
I do it better than anyone		Let me show you (Teach)
Follow the instructions		Follow me (Set the Example)

Stay tuned. There is much more to learn about thinking like a Leader in Lesson 3, "Manager vs. Leader: What's The Difference?"

Act like a Leader
When I was a Training Manager for a restaurant chain, I was sent to cover the 4th of July shift for another Manager at a nearby facility. It so happened that I had 2 Manager Trainees working with me, so I brought them along to continue their shift management training. As we walked in to take over leading the shift, I was informed that the July 4th fireworks were scheduled to begin at 9:15pm at the golf course just down the street. What I did not realize was that this restaurant was located next to a large vacant field, and when the golf course lot was full, hundreds of people swarmed that vacant lot to watch the fireworks. And they all wanted something to eat and drink! Things got pretty hectic as I, my two Manager trainees and a crew of 6 team members desperately tried to keep pace with the overflow crowd. I knew this would be a tough night, and to be honest, on the inside I felt like screaming. But as a Leader, I knew that that if I lost it, the entire team would fold, making the situation worse. What to do? I decided to "act" like we had everything

under control. My challenge was to keep everyone calm, moving, focused and yes, even smiling, for the guest. I knew that if I acted that way, so would the rest of my team. And it worked!

As the last of the guests were served, one of the Manager trainees approached me. "Everyone is saying they are glad you were here tonight. They say the other Manager has a hair-trigger temper, and if he were here, he'd be tossing stuff around and cursing under his breath. Everyone agrees you brought us through this night. Our question is: How did you do it? How did you manage to stay so calm and so in control in this crazy situation?"

I could see this was a real learning moment for my trainees, so when the time was right, we all sat down and discussed the evening's events. They were shocked to learn how I really felt (like screaming) during the chaos. "Well, you could have fooled us!" was their response, and that's when I knew I had accomplished what I set out to do that night.

I should mention that I'm not suggesting you try to change who you are. You can still be yourself and display a confident, professional image by looking, thinking and acting like the Leader you want to be. You can and should, display yourself with confidence as if to say "I'm your Leader, you're in good hands, follow me."

President Bill Clinton once said *"People will follow a Leader who is strong but wrong before they will follow a Leader who is weak but right."* Clearly, he is referring to perception. If your team perceives you to be a strong Leader through your appearance, actions and words, they will follow you to the ends of the earth and beyond – even when things go wrong, which is, as I discovered, the most important time for them to follow you!

The Leader's Notebook

Key points to remember from Lesson 1:

- Be sensitive of how your words and actions are perceived by the team, because their perception is their reality.

- In your role as Leader, how you are perceived by others will first be measured by how you look, think and act.

- There are no mistakes, only lessons. When a mistake is made, consider the more positive outlook that it is a learning opportunity, a lesson to be learned. Apply this philosophy to your team as well as yourself.

Recommended Development Actions

Sharpen your leadership skills through these developmental actions:

- What do you want your Leadership Legacy to be? Write down what you would hope your team would say about you after you're gone. Use it as your leadership behavior guide to remind you of the expectations you set for yourself.

- Conduct a quick self-evaluation. Do you look, think and act like the Leader you hope to be? Decide what you may need to do differently to live up to the expectations of your team.

- Ask your team to complete a quick, anonymous leadership survey on you. Or better yet, sit down with each member of your team and ask, "As the Leader of this team, what can I do differently that will meet or exceed your expectations?"

- Talk to your supervisor or another trusted associate. Ask for some honest feedback on what they think you can do differently to improve your leadership perception.

LESSON 2

LEADERS ARE MASTER GARDENERS

"Gardening requires a lot of water - most of it in the form of perspiration."
Lou Erickson

My wife, Shelby, is a Master Gardener. When it comes to the garden, few people are as knowledgeable about plants, trees and flowers as her. She knows what each one needs in order to not only survive, but to grow and flourish. She understands that all plants are different – each having their own unique needs relating to the quantity of sunlight, amount of water, type of soil and ideal growing temperature. She also understands that gardening is not easy. It takes planning, hard work and persistence to grow a beautiful garden. I believe that a good Leader acts as the Master Gardener of people. As with tending to flowers and plants, a Leader needs to first understand, and then tend to, the unique needs of everyone on the team. As the team's Master Gardener, the Leader provides not only what they need to survive (a paycheck), but what they need to grow and prosper, such as work that is challenging, an emotionally supportive environment and opportunities to succeed and get ahead in their careers.

The most successful Leaders accomplish their organizational goals and objectives through the greatness of the team they have nurtured and developed. Learning who your team members are, what they want to become and what motivates them to be their best should be the center of your focus. Equally important is for you to understand "who you are". It is the first step in uncovering your leadership potential and developing your leadership style. This process is different for everyone. For some, completing a behavior survey that identifies leadership strengths and opportunities can be very helpful. For others, gaining feedback from mentors can prove to be valuable in the identification of leadership development needs. For me, it began with understanding my fears. Early in my career, I knew that good leadership was grounded in the building of successful relationships. But I was also honest with myself in realizing that building relationships was not my strong suit. In fact, I was terrible at it because I hated it.

As I began to ask why, I discovered that I actually *feared* becoming involved in personal relationships. Where did that come from? As I thought of my life growing up, I uncovered the answer – and it really didn't surprise me.

Fears, Lies and Truths About Our Human Connection

Like too many people, I grew up living my life in fear. I feared challenging authority. I feared sharing my opinion. I feared making decisions because I feared being wrong. I was fearful of developing friendships. I feared not being accepted by others. And I feared being alone, forgotten and of looking stupid. In a nutshell, I was taught to fear people. As members of a highly dysfunctional family, my sisters, brother and I were taught the same lesson: *Children should be seen and not heard.* This archaic parenting philosophy was the cornerstone of my upbringing and, through it, my parents masterfully brain washed us to believe the "4 Don't"s of personal relationships:

1) <u>Don't</u> waste your time caring about people or their problems.
   Other people could care less about you and your problems.
2) <u>Don't</u> speak unless you are spoken to.
   Avoid embarrassing yourself – keep quiet.
3) <u>Don't</u> waste time forming friendships.
   People will always let you down. Trust no one.
4) <u>Don't</u> expect the best from others – assume the worst.
   Life is full of disappointments – prepare yourself for failure.

Not until my mid-twenties did I begin to understand the truths of our human connection. My Leadership Lesson was:

1) Caring about people is the glue that holds this crazy world together. You must show people you care about them.
2) Speak Up! Sharing your ideas and opinions will make the world a better place and you a better person.
3) Although we are far from perfect, our nature is more grounded in goodness than blended in betrayal. We all need each other. Trust people to do the right thing.
4) Everyone is successful at something. And even if you fail more times than you succeed at that something, the fact that you at least <u>tried</u> makes the effort a success in itself.

Here is a sample of what I have learned concerning the four truths:
Truth #1
Caring about other people is the glue that holds this crazy world together.

Leaders understand that their "business" is all about the well-being, development, skill and happiness of the team. Think about it: What business could survive without the people that make the product, provide service and clean up each day? Leaders care about their people because they understand their value to both the short-term and long-term success of the organization. The easiest way to show people you care for and respect them is by displaying simple acts of courtesy.

People often judge our leadership skill by the level of personal and professional courtesy we display. How you treat others both on and off the job speaks volumes about your values as a human being. And make no mistake, whatever role you are playing – Manager, Coach or Leader – everyone notices your behavior. Simple acts of common courtesy like saying please and thank you, opening a door for others, etc. demonstrate personal courtesies that all will notice, especially during times when you are under pressure.

Professional courtesies include addressing people you work with respectfully – even those you dislike or disagree with. Doing so sends the message that you are a professional Leader with a desire to forgo the political pettiness and gossip that others may thrive on. Like most people, I have had to work with others I disagreed with, and on a few occasions, really disliked. But you can dislike someone and still be respectful. Not always easy, but in doing so, you are proving to yourself and others that you are a professional Leader.

Truth #2
Sharing your ideas and opinions makes the world a better place.

Leaders speak up. They do not fear telling it like it is while showing respect for other people's opinions and ideas. Unlike Managers, whose job it is to *tell* people what to do, Leaders ask for help, solicit suggestions and ideas, make the decision and then set the decision into motion.

Truth #3
Although we are far from perfect, our nature is more grounded in goodness than blended in betrayal. We all need each other.
Trust people to do the right thing.

Consider this true story from Madrid, Spain, home to over 3 million people. Years ago, there was a young man named Paco. Living with his father, this 17 year-old with the common name was experiencing what many of us refer to as the "generation gap". Paco did not see eye-to-eye with his father on several things, and often they would find themselves having intense arguments. During one such exchange, young Paco stormed out of his father's house, vowing never to return. This was a scene often repeated in the past, but by day's end, Paco always found his way back home and he and his father would settle their differences. But this time was different. Paco failed to return home. After 3 days, his father was very concerned and began searching everywhere for Paco, but to no avail. After 7 days of searching for his son, he placed an ad in the personals section of the Madrid city newspaper. The ad read:

My Dear Son Paco;
Meet me on the steps of this newspaper office at 12 noon on Saturday. All is forgiven. I do care about you. Please come home. With Love, Papa.

It was reported that on the following Saturday, over 40 children gathered on the steps of the newspaper office at 12 noon; all named Paco, each searching for their father's forgiveness and love – all wanting to go home. This true story illustrates the power of one of our greatest human desires – to be cared about and loved by others.

We all need each other, and we all want to be needed. Leaders not only understand this, they use it as a foundation on which to build relationships. Leaders are givers. They understand that the greatest gift they can give is to show each member of their team that they are truly needed, valued and respected.

How Do Leaders Demonstrate This Caring Attitude?
As a young Leader, I cared about my team. I just didn't show it. And of course, that was the problem. If you want to *grow* people, you have to *know* people. Get to know your team. Learn about their families, what they like to do during their off time, their favorite TV shows. And above all, find out what motivates them to do their best work. And what is the best method to do this? Just ask them!

Once, my supervisor gave me that advice. So I started asking my team, "What motivates you to do a great job?" To my surprise, they were very candid with me. I expected everyone to say they wanted more money, and a few did. But most people made comments like, "I love it when I get to work on a special project, something other than my usual routine" and "I do my best when I get to teach new hires about the job." What I learned from that experience is that Leaders sometimes think they know the answers, or struggle trying to find answers, when the real answers are just a conversation away with the team members they serve.

Truth #4
Everyone is successful at something. And even if you fail more times than you succeed at that something, the fact that you at least <u>tried</u> makes the effort a success in itself.

What does it mean to be successful? Only you can answer that question. How you view yourself, what you want to accomplish and how you plan to accomplish it all matter. Leaders maintain a positive outlook and understand the bumps in the road to success are usually just that – bumps. And although these bumps may challenge their skill, real Leaders never allow them to alter their resolve.

The Question of Leadership

My personal story goes to the heart of the age-old question: **Are Leaders *born* or are Leaders *made*?** This has been a subject of debate in universities for years. The discussion has caused some people to believe that if they don't seem to have what it takes to lead a team, they are not a "born" Leader. Therefore, they should not try to advance into a leadership position. These are the people who never reach their full potential. And when a person fails to reach their full potential, it is a loss for not only the individual, but for their family and community as well. Know this: everyone, including you and me, has leadership potential that simply needs to be nurtured. Unfortunately, not everyone has the opportunity to unleash that potential. I certainly was not a born leader.

As you will see in the examples I share in the following chapters, I had to work at it. I read books, attended seminars and watched other good Leaders at work. I took all these learning opportunities and slowly began to develop my own leadership style. And through it all, I made my share of mistakes – or rather, I experienced some profound "lessons".

Ask any good Leader how they developed their leadership skills, and it is <u>highly</u> unlikely they will say, "Oh, I was a natural; I never had to learn about leadership, it just came to me." Most Leaders take the initiative to learn, grow and develop their skill. And most will tell you that they are still growing, learning and striving to be a better Leader for their team tomorrow. Are Leaders *born* or are Leaders *made*? What I have learned is that the answer is neither. Leaders are *nurtured*. Managers are *made*. Both are *born*.

It Takes a Lot of Work

When Lou Erickson said *"Gardening requires a lot of water - most of it in the form of perspiration"*, she was referring to the likes of the

LEADERS ARE MASTER GARDENERS

plant garden that my wife, Shelby, nurtures so well. Leaders are the Master Gardeners of people. The people that they nurture require a lot of tending, care and work. And, yes, just as gardeners do their share of "weeding" in the garden, taking out the weeds that threaten the health of the other plants, Leaders do the same as they build and nurture their team. Weeding is a small, albeit important, part of every Master Gardener's job.

Everything considered, the job of being a Leader is anything but easy. It takes time, commitment, patience and a ton of effort. But real Leaders love what they do because they understand the impact they have on the business and the lives of those they serve. When you ask a good Leader to describe the most time consuming part of their job, they often say it is the time they spend training and developing their team. And I have found that the best Leaders love every minute they spend cultivating that garden!

The Leader's Notebook

Key points to remember from Lesson 2:

- Leaders are not "born". They are nurtured and developed.

- Think of yourself as a Master Gardener of people. Constantly challenge yourself to find new ways to nurture, grow and care for every member of your team.

- We all need each other and we all want to be needed. Leaders not only understand this, they use it as a foundation on which to build relationships. Show your team you care about them and need them.

- Trust people to do the right thing. Remember that when given the chance, most of us will choose what's right for our team, our co-workers and our customers.

Recommended Development Actions

Sharpen your leadership skills through these developmental actions:

- Speak up and share your ideas. Call your supervisor this week and offer two suggestions. Ask that you be the one to take the lead in implementing the suggestions.

- Define success on your own terms. Find a mentor and with his/her help, set clearly defined goals and check your progress every 30 days. Make this a priority.

- To *grow* people, you have to *know* people. Get to know your team. Ask each person these 3 questions:

    - What motivates you to do your best work?
    - What would you like to learn?
    - What support do you need from me?

- When you get the answers, start preparing the development garden by taking action.

LESSON 3

MANAGER VS. LEADER: WHAT'S THE DIFFERENCE?

"Managers manage things, like processes and procedures. Leadership is about human experiences, not processes. Leadership is not a formula or a program, it is a human activity that comes from the heart and considers the hearts of others. It is an attitude, not a routine."

Lance Secretan

Would you prefer to spend the majority of your time working as a Manager or a Leader? The truth is that, in today's world, the most successful people not only *want* to do both, they *need* to do both. They manage when they must, but they also look for opportunities to lead. I have found that the most successful Managers exhibit strong leadership behaviors. Lesson 4 will focus on specific leadership behaviors, but first let's compare the roles of Managers and Leaders to see how they differ.

The Manager's Job
The #1 responsibility of a Manager is to solve problems, pure and simple. As you have already experienced, problems come in all shapes and sizes: from people, sales and profit problems to systems, operations and process issues. As a Manager, you get them all, in no particular order and often when you least expect them.

MANAGER VS. LEADER: WHAT'S THE DIFFERENCE?

Early in my career, I remember complaining to a fellow manager about some of the problems I was facing in my business. His response was, *"Well, if there weren't any problems, I guess they wouldn't need us Managers."* When we have our Manager hat on, that is what we do – we solve problems. Some people are reluctant to let go of their Manager hat. After all, managing problems successfully has probably got them where they are today. The issue is that managing in itself, while it gets you through the day, won't get you where you want to go in the future. Make no mistake; you will have plenty of opportunity to have your Manager hat on, solving all the day-to-day problems that arise in your business.

But while the "Manager" in you is busy putting out fires, the "Leader" in you should be asking questions – big questions – that get to the root cause of what started those fires to begin with.

The Leader's Job
When you act as a Manager, your #1 job is to solve problems.

As a Leader, your #1 responsibility is to build the business. Simply put, "building the business" means increasing sales and profits, causing the business to grow. It means being the Master Gardener of the Brand. People will sit up and take notice that you are the Brand caregiver, making the move from Manager to Leader - when your <u>behavior</u> changes. Some of the key behavior changes every Manager makes as they move to the leadership role include:

Manager	*moves to* ⟶	**Leader**
Manages a shift		Manages the Brand
Follows a process		Is a Learning Tour Guide
Hires people		Cultivates talent
Makes "to-do" lists		Makes "to-grow" lists
Corrects problems		Fixes the root cause

As you consider these behavior changes, think of what actions you need to take to implement them daily in your business.

Moving From Managing a Shift to Managing the Brand
Managers manage the actions of people. We tell them where to stand, what to do, how to do it. This is a needed function, as it organizes systems and processes while ensuring the team performs efficiently. If you have your "Manager hat" on right now, you are probably saying to yourself, "Yes, I do that, and I do it really well." You are a good – possibly great – Manager. Now switch to your "Leader hat". Ask yourself how you can better manage your Brand. Here's a good example of Brand Management.

The retailer Target attributes much of their success to the Store Leader's ability to train and develop a team of people who deliver their special Brand of Fast, Fun and Friendly service to every guest, every day. A District Leader once said to me, "Anyone can teach people to do a task like stocking shelves. But to keep the shelves full with well-merchandised, great products, tended by team members who are knowledgeable and go out of their way to be friendly and helpful to our guests – now that's managing the Brand."

Moving From Process Follower to a Learning Tour Guide
We love our checklists, don't we? And that's OK. They have their place in our Manager's tool box, so we have them hanging on clipboards all over the place. In addition to helping us manage processes, checklists help us remember all the complexities of our daily routines. They are simply a tool to help us execute a process. Leaders look at a checklist and the process as a learning opportunity because we view ourselves not as a process follower, but as a *Learning Tour Guide*. Think of what a "tour guide" does. They lead people along on an excursion, explaining the scenery, offering

explanations and answering questions. By the time the tour is over, people feel enlightened because they have learned something new. The next time you have to complete one of your operations checklists, make the move from Manager to Leader by giving a "learning tour" to someone on your team. Grab that clipboard and teach someone what you know about the process on the checklist. Then, let them do it!

Moving From Hiring People to Cultivating Talent
When a Manager needs to hire someone, it is out of necessity for the moment. That's about as far as the Manager thinks. A Leader will take a big picture approach, looking beyond the immediate need. For example:

Manager: "I have 2 service positions open. I need to hire two people for service."

Leader: "I have 2 service positions open. In 2 months, I will need to cross train them so they are able to move into production roles. I need to hire people that are capable of making that move. In addition, I need to look at how I will fill their service roles when I move them to production."
Look for much more on this topic in Lesson 5, "Building Your Team".

Moving From "to-do" Lists to "to-grow" Lists
When I was a multi-unit manager, I made daily "to-do" lists. It was the only way I could remember to do all the things I needed to accomplish. After taking a delegation workshop, I learned that delegating tasks would free up valuable time, allowing me to focus on the broader aspects of my multi-unit responsibilities, such as building the business.

I also learned that I could use delegation to develop my team members – to grow people – as well. I started making "to-grow" lists. Here's how my first two lists compared:

Manager's To Do List	Leader's To Grow List
Prepare the weekly sales report.	Teach Robert how to prepare the weekly sales report and have him do it twice a month.
Create action plan for unit 309.	Teach Sara the action plan process and ask her to create a plan for unit 309.
Present new sales reporting process to managers at the monthly meeting.	Teach Travis the new sales reporting process and have him present it at our next meeting.

Notice the word "teach" is prevalent on the Leader's to-grow list. As Leaders teach, people learn – their knowledge and skill become enhanced, thus aiding them in their current position while preparing them for future growth within your organization. It is a win-win for the team member, the Leader and the business.

Moving From Correcting Problems to Fixing the Root Cause
Every Saturday morning my wife and I go to a local supermarket to do our food shopping. On several occasions, we would search for our favorite coffee creamer in the dairy section, only to find the shelf empty. I would suggest stopping off at another store on the way home, but my strong-willed wife had other ideas. One

Saturday morning, straining to look through the empty dairy shelf, she said, "I can see the creamer in crates back there – they just haven't put them on the shelf yet." Ignoring my comment of, "Honey, I don't think you're supposed to go back there," she went marching off to find her coffee creamer and walked into the back storage room. Peering through the empty shelf to the backroom, I could see her pretty blonde hair bobbing up and down as she navigated around the tall crates, determined in her search. Finally, she found the liquid creamer and brought 3 bottles back to the shopping cart and her embarrassed husband. Our search for coffee creamer continued in this fashion for several weeks, until one Saturday morning visit when there were bright orange signs that had been posted on the doors leading to the backroom which read "Associates Only Please" – a clear message to my wife, and others like her, to stay out.

Of course, this did not deter my wife from her quest for creamer each week and, in fact, the problem of empty shelves persisted. I happen to know that, at this supermarket, they have department meetings every Monday morning. Based on the action they took to "solve" the problem, I can imagine the discussion that took place as they attempted to stop customers from wandering around in the backroom.

The Manager's Approach – Fix the Problem
General Manager: Anyone have a topic they want to discuss?

Dairy Manager: Yes, I need some help. It seems the customers keep wandering into the backroom looking for product.

Security Manager: Oh, we can't have that! Imagine our liability if one of them were to slip and fall. It's a lawsuit just waiting to happen!

General Manager: I agree. We need to keep those customers out of the backroom. Anyone have an idea?

Signing Manager: I know! We'll post signs that politely remind them to stay out. Most people obey signs.

Other Department Managers nod in approval as the Signing Manager begins designing his solution on bright orange paper.

Problem Fixed, Right?
Wrong! My wife continued to retrieve our coffee creamer from the backroom for the next 6 weeks, disobeying the bright orange sign and risking house arrest (or so I told her). It is likely that the signs slowed some of the customer traffic into the backroom, but was that the true problem, or was there more to the story? Had the Managers taken a leadership approach to problem solving, I can imagine their conversation and resulting actions would have been quite different. In the following scenario, they identify and fix the root cause of the problem by simply asking "Why" 5 times.

The Leader's Approach – Get to the Root Cause
General Leader: Anyone have a topic they want to discuss?

Dairy Leader: Yes, I need some help. It seems the customers keep wandering into the backroom for product.

Security Leader: Oh, we can't have that! Imagine our liability if one of them were to slip and fall. It's a lawsuit just waiting to happen!

General Leader: I agree. **Why (1)** do you think customers keep wandering in to our backroom?

Dairy Leader: Because the shelves are empty, but they can see the product in the crates in the back and they want the product.

General Leader: **Why (2)** do we have so many empty shelves in the dairy department every Saturday morning?

Dairy Leader: Because the dairy vendor delivers at 7:00am, but the stocking crew is not scheduled to start until 11:00am.

General Leader: **Why (3)** is the stocking crew scheduled four hours after the vendor delivers the product?

Dairy Leader: That's the way we've always scheduled them.

General Leader: **Why (4)** are we scheduling that way?

Dairy Leader: I guess when the vendor delivery schedule changed a few months ago, we did not adjust our crew schedule.

General Leader: **Why (5)** didn't we adjust the crew schedule?

Everyone looks around the room in silence.

General Leader: So, by adjusting the stocking crew schedule, we can get the product on the shelves immediately after the delivery?

Dairy Leader: Yes, and if the shelves are full, the customers won't need to go looking for product in the backroom. Problem solved!

Other Department Leaders nod in approval as the Signing Leader puts away his stack of bright orange paper.

Ask "Why" 5 Times – It's Easy and It Works!
The "5 Whys" is a technique used in the analyze phase of the Six Sigma methodology. It is not a new problem solving concept, yet I am surprised at the number of missed opportunities I see every day for people to use it. By repeatedly asking the question "Why" – five times is a good rule of thumb – you can peel away the layers of symptoms which can lead to the root cause of a problem. In my creamer experience, the Managers thought the problem to be solved was customers wandering around in the backroom of their store. In fact, that was merely a symptom of the real problem, which was product being out of stock. Although this technique is called the "5 Whys", you may find that you will need to ask the question fewer or more times than five before you find the core issue related to a problem.

The Leadership Lesson
When we are in our role as Managers, our job is to identify problems and fix them quickly. As Leaders, we should look deeper into the problem, identify and fix the root cause so the problem will not reoccur. Resolving the root cause of any problem will free up precious time to do more important business building activities. Yet many Managers will argue that they simply don't have the time to dig into the problem. John Wooden, the legendary UCLA basketball coach, said *"If you don't have time to do it right, when will you have time to do it over?"* Indeed, fixing problems <u>takes time</u>. Not fixing the root cause of a problem <u>wastes time</u> because you will find yourself fixing the same problem again and again.

MANAGER VS. LEADER: WHAT'S THE DIFFERENCE?

The Leader's Notebook

Key points to remember from Lesson 3:

- As a Manager, your #1 job is to solve problems.

- As a Leader, your #1 job is to build the business.

- Turn your weekly "to-do" list into your "to-grow" list.

- When faced with a problem, focus on getting to the root cause of the problem by asking "Why" 5 times.

- When making the move from Manager to Leader, begin by thinking in terms of how you will develop the team, build the business and manage your Brand.

Recommended Development Actions

Sharpen your leadership skills through these developmental actions:

- Create your Leader's "to-grow" list: Identify 3 team members on your staff and create a "to-grow" list for each of them.

- Select 2 team members and practice being their Learning Tour Guide on an activity of your choice. When selecting the activity, keep it simple and make sure it is an activity they can do unsupervised after you conduct the learning excursion.

- When faced with a problem, focus on getting to the root cause of the problem by asking "Why" 5 times. Make some quick notes to yourself of the why questions you ask so you can visually see how well the process uncovers the root cause. Then teach this process to your leadership team.

LESSON 4

KEY LEADERSHIP BEHAVIORS

"There are two types of people in this world, givers and takers. The takers may eat better, but the givers sleep better."
                                    Danny Thomas
                           Entertainer and Founder of
                        St. Jude's Children's Hospital

The Fantastic Four
During my leadership seminars, I conduct an interesting activity. Students are asked to think of a Leader in their life (a parent, coach, teacher, friend, etc.) who has demonstrated great leadership behavior. Next, I ask them to list the characteristics of that Leader. In other words, if the person is such a great Leader, <u>what did they do</u> that impressed you so much? The students then brainstorm all the characteristics of a good Leader. Often the list grows beyond 20, but inevitably they select the following four characteristics as "mission critical" for great Leaders. I refer to them as "The Fantastic Four":

1) **Demonstrate Self Confidence, Courage and Integrity**
   Display confidence in your ability and decisions. Have the courage to do the right thing, especially in tough situations.

2) **Build Your Credibility by Establishing Trust**
Always be true to your word – do what you say you will do. Live the example that you want others to follow.

3) **Provide Crystal-Clear Communications**
Make certain that without exception, everyone knows the goals, the daily plan, the expectations of performance and the rules of engagement on the job.

4) **Constantly Develop the Team**
Create and maintain an environment that encourages team members to grow in their job. Create, review and update personal development plans every 6 months, at a minimum.

Demonstrate Self-Confidence, Courage and Integrity

Leaders Demonstrate Self-Confidence
When I was 13 years old, I played the position of Guard on my grade school basketball team. Although I did my share of bench warming, I got to play in several games and loved every minute of it. In those days, I was "that kid" – quiet, withdrawn, avoiding conflict at all costs. All lessons learned from my dysfunctional home life. However, when I got to the basketball court, I was a different person. I fell in love with being part of a team. I got involved, I helped my teammates and I contributed to a goal. I yelled, cheered and expressed myself in ways that even surprised the other kids. At a young age, I was learning what it meant to be part of a team, working with others towards a common goal and following the guidance of a "coach".

Our coach was Coach Johnson, a stereotypical grade school basketball coach. Bulky and balding, part coach, part father figure, he was a tell-it-like-is man who showed no mercy when you made a mistake, but had a way of making you feel like a million bucks when you made a good play. He provided everyone on the team a safe practice environment. One where we could learn, laugh and be the best players we could be without fear of embarrassment or harassment. Coach Johnson made a point to nurture my need to belong at every opportunity and I found myself to be a fast learner. It was during one of the final games of the season that I experienced a lesson in leadership, compliments of Coach Johnson.

The Big Game
This was an important game. If we won, we would go to the finals. Lose, and we go home empty handed, season over. Our little school had never won a championship and knowing the possibility existed was enough to send the imagination of this group of 8th grade boys into overdrive. But as precious minutes ticked away during the 4th quarter, we had a big problem. We were losing.

Albeit by 3 points, we could sense the opposing team was gaining momentum and our nervousness turned to self-doubt, causing us to make costly mistakes. I recall thinking, "I know I can beat that kid to the basket. I can score. I can help win this game – if only I were in the game!" I was aching – I mean physically aching – to get in and do my part to win this thing. However, I remained on the bench for nearly the entire game. The Coach did give me a few opportunities. In the 1st quarter, our star guard, Kevin, sprained his ankle. Wincing with pain, Kevin hobbled off the court as Coach Johnson yelled to me, "Olson, can you go in for Kevin?" "Yea, I think so," was my reply. Coach looked at me, frowning, quickly looked away and yelled, "Dave, go in for Kevin!" My heart sank.

During the 3rd Quarter, it happened again. Rodriquez fouled out. The coach scanned the bench. "Olson, can you go in for Rodriquez?" "Yea, I think so," was my reply. With a sour face, Coach

Johnson yelled, "Mark, go in for Rodriquez!" I could not believe it! Only minutes left in the game and I have yet to touch the ball!

And then it happened. Paul fouled out and was ejected from the game. "This is my chance!" I said to myself. Coach Johnson, nearly breathless from his constant shouting, glared at me once again and asked, "Olson, can you go in for Paul?" With the crowd roaring in the background, I jumped from the bench and screamed, "Yes, I can! Let me in the game!" Sweat now pouring down the side of his face, Coach Johnson smiled and calmly replied, "Well now, if you would have said that the first time I asked you, I would have put you in the game sooner! Now get in there for Paul!"

The Leadership Lesson
During the final seconds of the game, I made the winning basket as I knew I would, and our team went on to the finals. More important than winning the game, I learned something at a tender age that some people never learn during their lifetime. *If you want to be a Leader – if you want to make a difference – you have to get yourself in the game.* Speak up. Tell people what you want, and then go for it. Express confidence in your abilities, even when you hear those little voices of self-doubt. Good coaches and Leaders always display a positive attitude and are the first to stand up and shout, "Yes, I can! Let me in the game!"

Leaders Demonstrate a Courageous "I Can Do That" Attitude
The most effective Leaders inspire other people to action, and that inspiration comes from demonstrating an attitude of "I can do that". A perfect illustration of the power of this positive and inspiring attitude can be found in the story of my grandparents, Rudolf and Lydia Rochau, who came to America from Germany in 1925.

Aboard the S.S. Republic November 1925
Left to Right: Heidi, Lydia, Alvin, Rudy

Lydia and Rudy Rochau
Kenosha, Wisconsin 1974

Rudolf "Rudy" Rochau was a man driven by the dream of a better life for his family. Married with two young children, this veteran of World War I dreamed of going to America, the land of opportunity. Germany had changed after the war. Rudy sensed more change was on the horizon, and it would be initiated by a young man promising a new era of German superiority – an awkward little fellow named Adolf Hitler. One day, Rudy rushed home to tell Lydia he had made up his mind. They were going to America, to settle in a small town near Lake Michigan called Kenosha, Wisconsin. Lydia listened respectfully to Rudy as he explained the details of their upcoming journey. Finally, Rudy paused and asked, "Well, what do you think?" Lydia began cautiously. "Let me see if I understand what you are suggesting. First, we will need to sell most of our belongings to purchase tickets for the two week boat trip to America with our two small children in tow. When we arrive in America, and assuming we are allowed to remain in the country, we will live in an unknown place for an unknown about of time. Then, somehow – we don't know exactly how – we will travel 900 miles from New York City to Kenosha, Wisconsin. Maybe by bus, maybe by train, or perhaps we'll walk – who knows? Once we arrive in Kenosha, we will find an unknown place to live, get unknown jobs with an unknown business, put our children in good schools we can only hope exist, and live happily ever after." A short pause, and then the question, "Rudy, do you *really* believe we can do this?"

My grandfather grinned, laughed and simply replied, "Yes, we can do this!" And with that, their journey to America began.

The Leadership Lesson – Grandma Was Right
Despite all the uncertainties faced by my grandparents, they – like millions of other immigrants – mustered up all the courage and attitude they could and did exactly what they set out to do. Rudy and Lydia settled in Kenosha, Wisconsin and raised their children;

my mom, Heidi, and my uncle, Alvin. Through his persistence, vision and courage, my Grandfather's hope for a better life for his family came to be. They truly lived the "American Dream", working for over 40 years at the same company before retiring in 1965, enjoying 53 years of marriage, 8 grandchildren and a host of great-grandchildren. My grandmother was fond of recounting this story and of reminding us: *"You know it really is true: When you believe you can do something, say out loud 'Yes, I can do this!' and you'll be half-way there!"* Here's what I have learned; as with so many other things, Grandma was right.

Having self-confidence is a key starting point in your leadership journey, but it is only one component. In the end, it will be your behavior – the actions you take – that will cause you to be recognized as a true Leader worth following.

Leaders Demonstrate Integrity
I was nervous and for good reason. My new supervisor, Garcie, was the type of boss you did everything in your power to avoid having a conflict with. He had a reputation for having quite a temper and I feared I was about to get a taste of it. I had just completed calculating the weekly performance numbers and they were not good. In fact, food efficiency was calculated at a dismal 88.2%. This was far below the 97% Garcie expected, so I knew he would not be happy. Before calling him, I anticipated his reaction and prepared my response, which was truthful and simple. I had made several bad decisions that affected the number. There were other reasons as well, but the bottom line was that I blew it and I was accountable. As I dialed his number on the telephone, I thought I was well prepared with my facts and explanations. In actuality, I was completely unprepared for what happened next.
Reading off the weekly numbers, the one I was dreading to report came closer. Finally, the moment came. The words slowly rolled

off my tongue. "Food efficiency is eighty - eight - point - two - percent." After a short pause, his temper exploded. "What the hell, Ben…how can that be?" I explained myself as best I could. "That number is not right," he said. I assured him the number had been triple checked and, unfortunately, it was accurate. He countered with, "That number is not right. I won't accept it. *Get me the right number. I don't care how you do it.*" With that, he hung up.

Was Garcie actually suggesting that I fake the number? I called another manager and shared my story. "What should I do?" I asked. The manager said, "He's wants a better number. Your only choice is to give him what he is asking for. Join the club Ben; we've all had to do it." I felt I had another choice. Leadership is a choice. I chose not to lie. I called Garcie back.

"Do you have a better number for me now?" He asked. "No, Garcie, the number is the same, 88.2%. I know you're disappointed. I am too. I guess I am most disappointed in myself. I take full responsibility for the decisions that I made that caused the efficiency to be so low, but the number is accurate and I don't see how I can change it without falsifying the weekly report." After a long pause, in an eerily calm voice, Garcie asked, "Do you like working here, Ben?" "Yes, of course I do," I replied. "Then call me back with the right number." Click. He hung up on me.

This thinly veiled threat that I could lose my job over the issue did not go unnoticed. Although I did like my job, I did not particularly like working for Garcie, but I had a family to support. I began to think about the process required to change the number, which included altering other numbers to make the 88.2% come out "right" to 97%. It was then I made my decision. I called Garcie back. "Now, what's the number?" he asked with a sigh. "Well, it's the same as it was the last two times we talked, 88.2%. And if you want to fire me for that, go ahead. I probably deserve it for the bad decisions I made that caused the problem. But I won't falsify the numbers." Click.

I hung up on him.

We never spoke about the conversation again. I was not fired, but he did treat me differently from that point on – with more respect.

Are You a Giver or a Taker?
The entertainer Danny Thomas once said: *"There are two types of people in this world, givers and takers. The takers may eat better, but the givers sleep better."* From a leadership standpoint, Garcie proved to be a "taker". He took what he wanted from his managers with little thought to the consequences or the impact of his words and actions. It was all about him; his career, his ambitions, his goals and his results.

The Leadership Lesson
I have learned that the best Leaders are "givers". They give of themselves to their people. They give their talent, expertise and wisdom as they strive to develop their teams to be the best at what they do. Leaders set the best example by demonstrating their character through the words they speak and the actions they take.

Build Your Credibility by Establishing Trust

Personal credibility is the very foundation of effective leadership. Credibility is earned and the way to earn it is to simply do what you say you will do. I am constantly amazed at the number of Managers who routinely make commitments and then break them. Then they are surprised when the team lacks motivation, team members don't perform to their potential and no one gives them respect. No one will ever respect you simply because you are the "Manager" or "Team Leader". Team members don't respect job titles; they respect the person who holds the title.

The Banking of Trust
In many ways, credibility and trust go hand-in-hand. For example, if you want to build trust, start by being true to your word. Doing what you say you will adds to your credibility, which in turn builds trust. Earning a person's trust is like earning and spending money. When you make a decision that builds trust, coins get added to your pocket. When you make a poor decision that removes trust, you have to pay out. As new Leaders, we all start out with the same amount of coins (trust) in our pocket. The banking of trust works like this: We can make deposits (a sincere and specific compliment) – we can make withdrawals (break an agreement) and we can borrow on credit (I promise it won't happen again). In the end, as in banking, if we pay out more than we put in, we go broke.

Demonstrate Credible and Trusted Behavior
Gaining the trust of your team is not easy to do. Far too many Managers fail to build trust because they are "I" centered. For the "I" centered Manager, every decision revolves around questions like: "What will this do for me? How will this help me get what I want?" They allow personal ego and a quest for power to steer their decisions. "I" centered Managers are focused on themselves, not on the team. And when you are not focused on your team, you are not leading. Of course, we're human beings and we all have an ego to manage, but the best Leaders keep their egos in check because they spend their time focused on their team, not themselves.

Beware the Braggers
Beware of people that tell you over and over how trustworthy they are. Remember, leadership is more about what you do than what you say. We are measured by others on our actions and the results

of our actions. I have noticed that the best Leaders *talk less* and *do more*. I have also noticed that people who constantly tell you how good they are at something are usually saying so to convince themselves as much as others. I once had a supervisor who would boast of how he cared for the team. He was fond of reminding people how dedicated he was to them, taking pride in treating each person with respect and so on. At first, we all bought into his talk, until his actions told a very different story.

A Withdrawal from the Bank of Trust
As a regional team leader, I was excited to get my annual performance review. I had tracked my results carefully and, although the past year had been filled with some huge challenges, I exceeded all of my performance goals. In fact, I was expecting to receive one of the best performance reviews of my career. Because my new supervisor, Matt, was out of state, he decided to conduct my performance review discussion over the phone, promising to send me a copy of my review in advance. He never did. When I mentioned I did not have my copy to follow along with, he apologized and explained that he would read the review over the phone and send me the copy to sign later. As our discussion began, I immediately sensed something was wrong. None of the performance ratings were an accurate reflection of the work I had done. He stated how disappointed he was in my performance, going on to cite specific data from a project that I had no part in.
It was then I knew he was reading from another team member's review! After a minute, I interrupted him. "Matt, I'm sorry but none of what you are saying makes any sense to me. Are you sure you are reading from my performance review form?" I could hear him fumbling with papers and then he said, "Oh, I'm sorry, I goofed! You're right; this is not your review. Wow, I don't understand how that happened! I'll find your review, send it to you right away, and we'll schedule another call to discuss it." Since he had failed on a promise already, I was

not at all surprised that he failed to send me a copy of the review "right away". Nor did he ever reschedule the call as promised. Instead, after several reminders from me and waiting nearly a month, I received my annual performance review in the mail, with a note asking that I sign and return it as soon as possible – no doubt, in order for him to make a filing deadline with his boss. I did receive a well-earned and significant increase in pay, but the extra money never compensated me for the lack of trust I felt for the man. All this from the bragger who loved to assure everyone how dedicated he was to treating his team members with respect. Through his actions, he earned a zero credibility rating from me and the rest of his team.

Got a Dent in Your Credibility Armor?
Occasionally, even the best Leaders will slip on the wet pavement of broken promises, damaging their credibility. There is an old saying that reminds us that one slip up doesn't mean the end of your career. *"Just because you have lost your way doesn't mean your compass is broken."* In other words, when stuff happens, don't quit. Your moral compass is still working; you may have just lost your way by making a bad decision. Get up, dust yourself off, and get on with the business of leading. By showing people you have the courage to accept responsibility for your decisions and are willing to continue on, you are actually taking the first step of resetting your compass to rebuild your credibility. And I can promise, you'll find your way again.

Credibility is Anchored by Trust
Credibility builds trust. Lack of credibility destroys trust. The degree of loyalty, commitment and productivity you can expect from your team will depend on how credible they feel you are as their Leader. That's why it is no understatement to say that credibility – which is anchored by the trust between people – is one of the most critical foundations of leadership.

Provide Crystal-Clear Communications

Lack of providing clear communications has resulted in the demise of many Leaders. The rule of thumb in effective communication is simple: Communications should be so clear that everyone can understand the message. Here are some actual communications I have seen in my travels. Which one is crystal-clear?

Manager Note

NOTICE TO ALL EMPLOYEES:

Failure to follow the attendance policy will result in

disciplinary action.

Signed,

The Manager

Leader Note

How Do You Spell R-E-S-P-E-C-T?

Be on time to work and

leave your station 100% ready for the next shift!

Signed,

The Leader

In the "Manager" communication, several questions immediately come to mind. First, what exactly is the attendance policy and second, precisely what disciplinary action will be taken? In addition, the Manager's note expounds a threatening tone of "do-this-or-else".

The Leader's message is very different, offering 2 specific behavioral expectations: be on time to work and leave your station ready for the next shift. It also reveals the result: doing so will show your respect for fellow team members. In addition, the tone of the Leader's note is much more positive than the Manager's.

We have all heard (and probably used) the saying *"Everyone needs to be on the same page."* Exactly what does that mean? It means that everyone understands the detail of the communication. Communicating expectations in a clear way ensures everyone is on the same page.

Show Them the Page
During a discussion with a client, she mentioned to me that she had to give disciplinary warnings to several employees for violating the dress code policy. Her exact words were, "I can't seem to get everyone on the same page when it comes to the dress code." I asked where the policy was posted. She responded it was not posted, but that everyone had to sign the dress code policy when they were hired and a copy was tucked away in their personnel file. Of course, many of the employees signed that policy a year or more ago. With no other reference point, how can one legitimately require employees to be aware of (and remember) all the details of the policy? So I suggested something I had learned from international consultant Pam Boyd: *If you really want everyone to be on the same page, you have to show them the page.* "Let's post a copy of the policy on your bulletin board and, throughout next week, review it with each employee. Have them sign the posted policy to verify you discussed it with them and that they understand it. Since you will be speaking directly one-on-one with each person, it will also be the perfect time to address any specific questions they may have." The client took my recommendation and two weeks later telephoned to thank me for the suggestion. There were no more dress code violations. Showing them the page was, in fact, her first step in providing crystal-clear communications on the topic of the dress code policy and ensured everyone was indeed on the same page.

How You Say It Matters Almost as Much as What You Say
Abraham Lincoln, John F. Kennedy, Martin Luther King Jr., Reverend Jesse Jackson, Ronald Regan and Hillary Clinton all come to mind when we think of great communicators. So I did some research on each person and discovered they all had a few things in common. First, they understood that getting other people to listen to you is not an easy task, but a requirement if you expect people to follow your lead. Secondly, they all spoke clearly, using common words without street slang. For example, notice they used "Yes" and "No" instead of "Yeah" and "Nah". They all worked at expanding their vocabulary. And finally, they were all well-read. They were in the habit of reading out loud to hear and practice their delivery of not only the core message of their speech, but vocal tone and pronunciation as well. They understood the power of the spoken word in relation to being an effective communicator.

Abraham Lincoln – the Crystal-Clear Communicator
"It is rather for us to be here dedicated to the great task remaining before us – that from these honored dead we take increased devotion to that cause for which they gave the last full measure of devotion – that we here highly resolve that these dead shall not have died in vain – that this nation, under God, shall have a new birth of freedom – and that government of the people, by the people, for the people, shall not perish from the earth."
Excerpt from the Gettysburg Address by Abraham Lincoln

The Gettysburg Address is one of the greatest examples of the power of delivering a clear message. President Abraham Lincoln gave the 2 minute speech on November 19, 1863. Containing only 10 sentences, it has continued to inspire millions of people for more than a century. There was another speaker at the event, Edward

Everett, who, by the way, was considered to be one of the greatest public speakers of his time. He spoke just before the President for nearly 2 hours on the same topic. Over 150 years later, which speech is remembered? Lincoln's, of course. And why do you think that is? Because his 10 sentences contained the very essence of the message he wanted to convey and nothing more. It was direct and to the point, using language that everyone at the time understood. Even Edward Everett acknowledged the power of the President's speech. In a note to the President the day after the event, Everett wrote: *"I should be glad, if I could flatter myself that I came as near to the central idea of the occasion, in two hours, as you did in two minutes."* A humble servant Leader, President Lincoln graciously replied, *"In our respective parts yesterday, you could not have been excused to make a short address, or I a long one. I am pleased to know that, in your judgment, the little I did say was not entirely a failure."* Although he received great reviews from countless others, Lincoln himself actually thought his short speech failed to deliver his message, and would soon be forgotten. So one can only imagine President Lincoln's surprise if he were to learn that his Gettysburg Address became the benchmark example of a crystal-clear communication, finding its place in American history as one of the most powerful speeches ever made.

My Communication Wake-Up Call
Louie was a cook, and a darn good one at that. He was fast, productive and detail-oriented. Louie was also 16 years old and full of life. Everyone enjoyed being around Louie. He was fun-loving, smart, and always sporting a sardonic smile that made you wonder what he was up to. All that said, he had one big problem – he could not seem to get to work on time. He was late so often that the running joke was he operated not on Central Standard Time, but on "Louie Time". It seemed that no matter how I coached, counseled or threatened, he continued to report for work in his time zone,

KEY LEADERSHIP BEHAVIORS

according to his clock. A good Leader would have simply followed the company attendance guidelines and fired him months earlier. But I was inexperienced both as a coach and as a Leader, lacking the courage to confront the problem. I found it easier to make empty threats and *hope* his behavior would change. The change I hoped for never materialized.

One very busy afternoon, Louie was scheduled to start his shift at 4:00pm. As usual, he was late. The time continued to pass and the restaurant became extremely busy. During the heat of the rush hour, one of the cooks said to me, "Well, it looks like Louie blew us off again, not that you'll do anything about it." Clearly, this was a dig at my inability to deal with the attendance problem. I lost my temper and shouted, "Well, that's it! When he shows up, he's fired! I've had it with that kid!" I had made up my mind. It was time to get tough and show the rest of the team I was serious. As the evening wore on, I announced my intentions – several times, in fact – to fire Louie. I was going to set an example and I wanted everyone to know it.

At least that is what I thought. Instead, I was about to receive a lesson in leadership I would never forget.

Around 9:00pm, Louie's mother called to say that he had been in a car accident that afternoon. Street racing with friends, he lost control of his car and, as it left the road, it hit several trees and rolled end-over-end. He was killed instantly. Time seemed to stand still as I struggled to find the right words. I could not believe what I was hearing. Finally, I expressed my sympathy and asked that she keep us informed about the pending memorial service. I went on to say how Louie was loved by everyone who worked with him, and how he would be missed by all, to which his mother replied, "I know…..I'll miss him too," crying uncontrollably as she hung up the phone.

Reflecting on my evening rants of "I've had it with that kid", I felt both ashamed of my behavior and deeply saddened by Louie's death. And now, I had to relay this tragic news to my team. We were just about to close the restaurant, so I simply told them that I wanted to have a brief meeting before we left for the night. Because of my prior threats, everyone assumed I'd have something to say about firing Louie. Instead, we cried and hugged and shared our stories about the kid with the quirky smile who really was fun to be around, even when he operated on "Louie Time".

The Leadership Lesson
This sad event actually became my wake-up call. From a communications standpoint, I failed to communicate the standards of attendance to Louie and the rest of the team. To add to that problem, I failed to take corrective action concerning his behavior. Remember, I was taught by my parents to avoid conflict. Like anyone who avoids conflict, my solution was to just "hope" his behavior would change. Of course, that did not work and it never does. After the funeral, I did a lot of reflecting and reevaluated my leadership skills. From that experience I made the following commitments to myself:

- I would no longer avoid performance issues, but rather tackle them head on as they occurred. I learned how to look people in the eye, and calmly, respectfully say: "If you don't change your behavior, I will have to take disciplinary action that may lead to the termination of your employment. Whether or not it leads to that is entirely up to you."

- During times I felt frustrated, under pressure or angry, I would force myself to smile and project a calming influence so that my team would perceive I was in control and

KEY LEADERSHIP BEHAVIORS

we would get through the challenge together. I would "act" like the Leader I wanted to be.

- Every written communication I produced would be positive in its tone and crystal-clear in its message.

I still strive to follow these commitments every day and I believe they have made me a better Leader, coach and communicator.

Constantly Develop the Team

Several times during my career, I accepted new assignments that challenged my abilities to the core. In one situation, I recall facing more problems than you could shake a stick at. Sales, profits and guest transactions were all far below goal. The restaurant was poorly maintained and dirty. The team was poorly trained, unmotivated and had largely been left on their own. Service and production process issues caused more than our share of guest complaints. And the management staff was dysfunctional due to a lack of focus, communication and training. Where to begin? A Manager focusing on the tasks would answer, "Let's begin with cleaning the place up, fix the equipment, paint the walls" and the like. But I understood that to make long-term, positive changes, I needed to focus on the team and move from my Manager mindset to that of a Leader. My approach was:

Manager *moves to* ➡	**Leader**
Clean the equipment	Teach cleaning program
Write up poor performers	Re-train on the basics
Communicate rules	Communicate goals
Fire the Asst. Managers	Develop the Asst. Managers

However, this move was not recognized immediately by my superior. I remember she came in for a status visit. "Why haven't we cleaned that wall yet? I thought you were going to get that done yesterday." I moved into my Leader's role and responded, "Because I spent the day training the service team to reduce packing errors that are causing most of our guest complaints. I'll get to the wall tomorrow." Realizing I actually had my priorities in line, she nodded with approval and asked for an update on my training plan.

Five Keys of the Team Development Process
Leaders provide a continuing process of team development that actually begins before the team member is hired and continues long after. I have found that the most successful teams are developed by Leaders who consistently deliver on these five keys:
Establish a Safe Environment, Maintain Self-Esteem, Provide Consistent Training, Offer Development Opportunities and Be Future-Focused.

Establish a Safe Physical and Emotional Environment
Physical safety and security on the job is now the number one concern for the vast majority of American workers. At one time, it could almost go without saying that providing a physically safe work environment was a paramount expectation, a real no-brainer. Workers assumed leadership would provide a safe place to work. How hard could that be? Unfortunately, we see today's news filled with stories of workplace violence, school shootings and road rage incidents that cause us to shake our heads in disbelief. Physical safety in the workplace is a topic in itself for another book. For our purpose, I'll sum it up this way. As Leaders, our responsibility is three-fold. First, we are accountable to know, communicate and implement all company guidelines relating to workplace safety. Secondly, leadership is accountable to report and correct potential hazards before they become issues. And finally, it is our

responsibility to take action as required by law and/or company policy. The bottom line is: Keeping the team safe and secure is priority one for every Leader.

Emotional safety relates to our personal comfort level. No need to fear sexual harassment, bullying and the like. The team feels their "space" is secure and free of such negative forces. The Leader is the person who ensures this to be so. For many people this emotionally safe environment may be the very reason they come to work. I once had a team member say to me, "I love working here." When I asked her why, I assumed she would say it was due to her pay or benefits but instead she replied, "I have a lot of stuff to deal with in school and at home. When I come here (to work) I feel safe from all that. People here are friendly and they treat me with respect."

Maintaining Self-Esteem Begins With Maintaining Self-Respect
There are many pieces to the puzzle of what causes people to take pride in their work, but most are centered on the belief that performance improves when we are proud of what we produce, have a sense of personal accomplishment and we just plain feel good about ourselves. I have always believed that self-pride begins with a person's self-perception. My formula for getting my team members to be proud of themselves and the work they accomplished was actually pretty simple; Look Good = Feel Good = Do Good. In other words, if we look good, we will feel good. And if we look and feel good, we will do well.
Making people feel good about themselves begins with simple things, such as providing them with a clean, properly fitting uniform.

New Uniforms = New Attitudes
In one operation that I was assigned, I could see from day one that none of the crew cared much about their job, our Brand or

themselves for that matter. All it took was one look at them to understand why. Their uniform shirts were stained and torn; slacks did not fit properly and were in poor repair and name badges looked as though they were handwritten by a fifth grader. Collectively, this team looked like a rag-tag group of nomads and that's also how they were behaving. I knew that if I could make them feel better about themselves, their performance would begin to turn around, too. I carefully made a list of uniform needs, being certain I was ordering the correct size for each team member. Two weeks later the uniforms arrived. I announced a "grab a donut and your new uniform" meeting for Saturday morning at 8:00am. To my surprise, all 34 employees were lined up at the door at 7:45am, waiting for my arrival, some free donuts and a chance to gain back their self-pride via a new, clean, properly fitting uniform. I will never forget the smiles the new uniforms brought to their faces, nor one young lady's comment that was shared by several others as she admired her new look: "Wow, I feel like a whole new person!" Of course, this event did not fix all the issues we had yet to face together, but everyone, including the area supervisor, customers and some of their parents, noticed the attitude change in each team member after that day. It made my job of leading the necessary changes a bit easier because they started to care about themselves, each other and the Brand. And all it took were some new uniforms!

There's No Magic Formula for Great Performance
Here's a question I am often asked during my coaching seminars: *How do you get people to do what you want them to do? Is there a secret, some kind of magic formula?* In the end, it really all comes down to this: People produce better results when they feel good about themselves. Experience has shown me that if we create an environment of respect, trust and commitment, we are more likely to get good (if not great) performance from our team. This is one of the universal truths of leadership. Imagine what your job would be

like if each member of your team, including your leadership team, were **great** performers – being the very best at what they do.

When do we do our best work? Many people will say when they are feeling good, happy and confident in their ability. Maintaining a positive work atmosphere in your business – one that builds the employee's self-esteem – will lead to trust and foster long-term commitment.

Building Self-Esteem Begins With Respect
For many people, their self-esteem comes from the respect others show them. The first rule about respect is **WS-GS** – if you **Want Some**, you have to **Give Some**. Respect can be defined as "how I feel about myself when I'm around you." Everyone wants to feel that they matter – that they are important to someone. Respect leads to trust. If you demonstrate respect for someone, you are building their self-esteem and they will learn to trust you. What a Leader gives to build self-esteem, trust and commitment, they receive back from the team in loyalty, commitment and great performance.

Tell Me About Your Team
As the new Market Leader, I was making the rounds visiting my leadership teams for the first time. Prior to visiting with one Manager, my boss had warned me, "She's on her way out. You'll need to replace her, so you can start planning for that now." Of course, I wanted to assess the situation for myself, so I paid this Manager a visit. I have found that you can tell a lot about a Leader if you ask them to tell you about the people that report to them, so my practice was to ask questions about the team. When I asked this Manager to tell me about her team, she began by saying, "Let me tell you, this is a tough group of people. They don't show me any respect." "I'm sorry to hear that," I responded. "Tell me about

that young man over there." "Oh, he's a real loser; I can't believe I hired him," she said. "What about the young lady over there?" I asked. "She is worthless," was the response. "And the gentleman over there – tell me about him." "Dumb as a bag of hammers!" was her reply. At this point I stopped her and said, "You've told me two things so far that are really disturbing. One, your team does not respect you. And two, it's clear that you don't respect the team." We proceeded to sit down to have a private conversation about **WS-GS**.

The Leadership Lesson
To be honest, my first thought about this person was, "My boss was right. She is an 'I' centered Manager who has no respect for her team. She will have to go!" But I caught myself, realizing that this is the "disposable" thought process of a Manager, not the people growing actions of a Leader (more on this in Lesson 5). I knew it was my responsibility to help grow this individual, yet it also was my duty to ensure my Leaders were treating their teams with respect. As we sat down, I asked, "Have you had the chance to read the book In Search of Excellence by Tom Peters and Nancy Austin?" She shook her head no. "Well, in their book they offer a simple and true definition of coaching. If you want to think about what it means to be a Leader, you could insert the word 'Leadership' for the word 'Coaching' in the same statement. If you did, it would read:

"Leadership (Coaching) is not about memorizing techniques or devising the perfect game plan. It's about really paying attention to people – really believing in them, really caring about them, really involving them."

I went on to ask, "What does this statement mean to you?" She was quiet for a minute, thinking about what I had just said. Her response reinforced my belief that there was a Leader hidden within this Manager. She said, "I guess you're actually showing me what being a Leader is really about, by caring enough to even have this conversation with me."

My boss was surprised to learn that I did not fire her. Instead, over the next several months, I continued to work with her, as she took ownership to make her move from Manager to Leader.

Provide Consistent Training
Zig Ziglar once said *"The only thing worse than training employees and losing them, is not to train them and keep them."*

In several of my experiences, I have found that my well-intentioned predecessors were great trainers – at least in their minds. They "trained" everyone to do a little bit of everything. However, all that did was lead to situations where everyone knew how to do everything, but no one knew how to do any one thing right.

And that left me with an entire team of people making a lot of mistakes, resulting in production errors, slow service and guest complaints. Leaders create documented training plans that indicate who will be trained, what they will be trained on, when they will be trained and by whom. And as we will discuss in Lesson 5, Leaders will conduct the beginning of every training session to ensure their "people garden" is being properly cared for.

Offer Development Opportunities
In one situation, I discovered I had inherited an entire team of people who had been in position for some time, yet their performance was inconsistent at best. It seemed as though they were tired and bored with their job. In fact, that was the real problem; it was just a "job" to many of them. So I set out to put some spark back into the team by offering development opportunities. I posted a

notice announcing that I would be conducting advanced training on a variety of topics for all who attended on Monday nights from 7:00pm to 9:00pm. All participants would be paid for their attendance, and this training would lead to advanced certifications, which in turn would lead to a pay increase. After I posted the notice, I was approached by a team member, Katie. "Let me get this straight," she said. "I show up on Monday night, you work with me on my station certification, I get paid for attending <u>and</u> I'll get a raise if I pass my certification?" "That's right," I assured her. "Plus you'll be able to work a new position, so you'll get to do something different for a change!" Katie walked away shaking her head, saying, "Yea, well, I've heard that one before." I later learned that the "Manager" before me had made several promises to conduct similar development sessions and failed to follow through. I could see the team lacked commitment in part due to the broken promises. He had emptied their "trust" bank account. It was now up to me to make some deposits.

All week I continued to talk up the Monday night development session. When the time arrived, I was excited to get started, but there was a small problem. No one showed up. Not one person. Undeterred, I spread the news that I would be holding another session the following week. This time, one person attended. And that's when it happened. Several team members on duty approached me asking what Katie and I were doing. I told them, "This is the development training I've been talking about. It's every Monday night and it's open to everyone." I could still sense their hesitation, but the following week I had 2 more team members attend. Before long, I had so many people attending the Monday night session that I enlisted the help of one of my assistant Leaders (who was on my "to-grow" list) to help out. Within 90 days, we had developed over 20 people, helping them grow into other positions. And, by the way, it was no coincidence that during this 90 day period, sales increased 11% over the previous year.

The Leadership Lesson
Providing development opportunities for your team will demonstrate respect, while building trust, self-esteem and personal commitment. It ignites a contagious spark that results in greater performance and higher morale within the entire team.

Create Your Vision – Later!
If you read other books about leadership (and you should!), you'll notice most of them have something to say about Leaders being the visionary of the business. They create a vision and work to get everyone on board to see it and work towards it. I can't argue the importance of this, but I can tell you that, if you are a new Leader, goal setting and action planning are steps you need to take before you put your visionary hat on. Here's why I believe this:

Have you ever been told of an upcoming change and found yourself saying, "They should have listened to me. I suggested that a year ago!" You are not alone. Many times great ideas are wrapped in a vision, suggested and discarded only to resurface and be implemented later. Why? It's all a matter of timing. Sometimes the answer is simply that your organization was not ready, even though you were. Leaders are often expected to set the vision for their organization and be the visionary as well, predicting the future. Truth is, more often than not, their guess of what the future holds is no more accurate than yours or mine.

The Leadership Lesson
Being a visionary is great and every business needs one. But being a visionary is not as important as being able to act on the vision.

So as a new Leader, it is best that you focus on the short term goals before you get into the science of creating a vision.

Be Future Focused
English politician Charles Buxton said, *"In life, as in chess, forethought wins."* In the game of chess, thinking ahead and pondering the "What Ifs" of your opponent's moves are critical elements to winning.

In some ways, leadership can be compared to the game of chess. Leaders are forward-thinking. They communicate, in crystal-clear fashion, exactly where the team is headed and what needs to be done to get there. I believe that 80% of our ability to achieve any goal requires planning for what lies ahead, while adjusting our game plan to what we have learned from the past. The remaining 20% requires us to get off our butt and just do it.

KEY LEADERSHIP BEHAVIORS

The Leader's Notebook

Key points to remember from Lesson 4:

- The most effective Leaders inspire people to action. They project an "I can do that" positive attitude.

- Speak up. Tell people what you want and then go for it. Express confidence in your abilities even when you hear those little voices of self-doubt.

- The best Leaders are "Givers". They give their talent, expertise and wisdom as they strive to develop their teams to be the best at what they do.

- Credibility is anchored by trust. The easiest way to earn trust and build your credibility with the team is to simply do what you say you will do. Don't focus on telling people how good you are – show them. Leaders *talk less* and *do more.*

- Do not ignore poor performance. Face performance problems head-on. Follow your company's policy and procedures regarding disciplinary actions consistently.

- Before taking any disciplinary action, be sure to get all the facts. Things are not always as they seem.

- Personnel performance issues <u>should not</u> be discussed with team members. Discuss only with your leadership team and your supervisor.

- To keep everyone on the same page, all communications should be concise, positive in its tone and crystal-clear.

- Maintaining a person's self-esteem begins with showing them respect. Respect is a two-way street. If you want some, you have to give some. (WS-GS)

- Self-Esteem: Look Good = Feel Good = Do Good

Recommended Development Actions

Sharpen your leadership skills through these developmental actions:

- Create a list of actions you can take that will inspire other people to do the right thing in challenging situations.

- Ask your team if they perceive you as a person who has an "I can do that" attitude. If the answer is anything less than "always", you have some work to do.

- If you want to make a difference, you have to get in the game. Tell your supervisor what you would like to be doing 2 years from now. Ask for help in accomplishing your goal.

- Imagine you are having a conversation with the late Danny Thomas and he asks, "Are you a giver or a taker?" How would you respond? What examples could you provide?

- Review your company's disciplinary procedures. Make sure they are communicated in crystal-clear fashion to all team members so that everyone is on the same page.

- Expand your vocabulary by learning new words and using them. Join an online "word of the day" club.

- Video record yourself telling a short story. Review the video, paying attention to the words you use, your facial expressions, tone of voice and message clarity. Are you a crystal-clear communicator?

- Enhance your knowledge of communication skills by attending a communication workshop or reading a book.

- Imagine that by accident your supervisor copied you on an email to her boss which contained a glowing report about your leadership skills. Write down what you think would be said in that email message. Next, determine what you need to do to make it a reality.

LESSON 5

BUILDING YOUR TEAM

"The basic building block of good teambuilding is for a Leader to promote the feeling that every human being is unique and adds value."

The Fundamentals of Building Your Team
As the Master Gardener of the team, Leaders understand the importance of the core fundamentals of team building. It begins with selection – hiring the right person for the job. Then, orientation – ensuring the new hire receives all the need-to-know information about the organization and the team they are joining. Next, provide great training and finally, offer future-focused development that will allow the individual to grow into other positions within the organization.

Your company has specific guidelines relating to interviewing and recruiting and I strongly recommend you follow them. As a Leader charged with building a high performing team, there are a ton of considerations – both legal and otherwise – in this process. Rather than review all the basics, I will leave that to your company training manuals. Instead, I offer my personal tips for you as a Leader that, in addition to your company guidelines, will help you select, orientate, train and develop a great performing team.

Selection: Know What You are Looking For

As every Human Resource professional will tell you, selecting the right person for the job is critical if your intention is to build a strong, high performing team. In my travels, I see Managers who hire the first person they interview just to fill the position. As with most things, Leaders take a longer view of the recruiting process. They are willing to search and wait as long as necessary to find and hire the right person. What's the "right person"? That is what you need to determine before you conduct any interviews. Prior to the interview, you should make a short list of the skills that you are looking for.

For example, let's say you are conducting interviews to hire a customer service team member. This is what your list may look like:

Position: Customer Service
Skills and abilities to look for during the interview:
- Naturally friendly, helpful behavior
- Smiles and can easily maintain a conversation
- Presents a positive attitude
- Presents clean/neat personal appearance
- Prior customer service experience a plus
- Ability to handle complaints professionally
- Works well with other members on a team
- Willingness to cross-train to another position within 6 months
- Schedule availability must include rotating weekend shifts

Assuming that the current personality of the team is what you are attempting to build on, an additional consideration is finding a candidate who will be a good "fit" with your current core team. A qualified candidate who is loud and overbearing, for example, will clash from day one with a team consisting of quiet, more serious-minded team members. The reverse is also true. If your core team consists of A+

personality types ("outgoing socialites", I like to call them), a quiet introverted person may not be the best candidate for the team. Your intention should be to hire a candidate who will complement – not clash with – the personality make-up of your existing team.

What You Can – and Can't – Teach People

As you review the list of skills and abilities, you should identify which are trainable and which are not. Once during a job fair, I sat in on an interview conducted by a department Manager. The candidate was applying for a customer service position. I noticed that the candidate did not smile once during the interview. She did not maintain eye contact with the Manager. She spoke very quietly and the Manager had to ask her to speak up several times because we could not hear the responses to some of our questions. Afterwards, I was surprised to learn that the Manager made the candidate a job offer. When I pointed out that the candidate did not smile or maintain eye contact and was very soft spoken, the Manager explained, "She will learn all of that during her training," to which I replied, "That's interesting, I did not know we had a class that taught people how to smile!"

You can teach people the mechanics of their new job. You can teach the new hire customer service team member how to follow service steps, handle complaints, answer the business telephone and complete service checklists. Even some aspects of personal appearance can be taught. Here's what you can't teach: You cannot teach a person to smile, to be friendly and courteous or to be helpful. Those are traits that either they have or they don't. If you do not observe these traits during the interview, it is very unlikely the person will change after they start the job. You can determine if a person is helpful by nature by asking a behavior example question.

Interviewer Statement: "Give me a recent example of a time when you went out of your way to help someone."

Candidate Response: "Well, yesterday as I was coming home from school, I noticed an elderly neighbor struggling with her grocery bags. I went over and helped her carry them to her apartment."

What This Response May Indicate: The candidate just told you they are alert to notice when other people need help and they took action without being asked. As a customer service representative, this individual is likely to behave the same way on the job. When they see a customer who needs help, they will naturally go to help them without being told to do so.

When People Show You Who They Are, Believe Them
My wife has long been fond of this quote and I have found it to be true on several levels in the business world. You can apply this to the interview process by simply observing and listening to your candidate. If our customer service candidate never smiled once during the interview, they are showing you who they are. Don't expect them to be smiling much towards your customers if you hire them.

How to Find Out Who They Really Are
A truism about human behavior is reflected in the saying, *"Past performance is an indicator of future performance."* What we have done in the recent past is likely how we will behave in the near future. Presenting hypothetical questions or asking for the candidate's philosophy will not tell you how they have behaved in the past. To find out who they really are, ask questions that target specific past behavior.

The difference between a hypothetical and behavioral question is:

Hypothetical questions begin with: "What would you do if...."
Behavioral questions begin with: "Tell me about a time when you...."

Knowing that prior performance is an indicator of future performance, we need to ask questions that will help us determine what the candidate has actually done, not what he would or should do. Asking a hypothetical question such as *"How do you think a Team Leader should deal with under-performing team members?"* will only tell us what the candidate's philosophy or opinion is.

Were You – or Were You Not – a Team Leader?
I was speaking with a candidate who had applied for a Team Leader position. He indicated he had previous experience building a high performing team and went into some detail of the team's accomplishments. It sounded good at first, until I realized he was speaking in generalities. I wanted to know exactly how he made his team so successful, so I asked a behavioral question.

"Tell me about a time when you had to deal with a team member who was under-performing. As the Team Leader, how did you deal with the situation?" The candidate said, "I strongly believe (his philosophy) that a Team Leader (speaking about a third party) needs to keep their team (not speaking about his team) focused on their responsibilities and help them achieve their goals." On the surface, that response sounds good, but it did not tell me what the candidate had actually done in the past to deal with under-performing people. As I pressed him to provide a more specific example, it came out that this person had never directed a team before, as he led me to believe at the start of our discussion.

Caution: Keep Your Interview Questions Legal
During the interview process, you must be careful not to ask illegal questions. These questions are likely listed in your company's interviewing guidelines and, again, I strongly recommend you read and follow them. A good rule of thumb to follow concerning interviewing

is that you should not ask any question that does not have a direct impact on the candidate's ability to perform the job. For example, "Are you married?" is considered an illegal question because a person's marital status has no bearing on their ability to perform the job.

Hire Candidates with the Future in Mind
When it comes to hiring and staffing, Leaders are future-focused. During the recruiting process, look for individuals who are capable to be cross-trained for other positions. Some Managers hire entire teams of individuals for specific positions, knowing up front that each person will never be capable of moving up or over to another position. This immediately stifles productivity and negatively impacts payroll costs, scheduling flexibility and can even affect team morale. Remember, Leaders are growers of people, and in order to grow people, you have to hire those who have the potential to grow within both the team and the organization.

Provide a Great Orientation and Initial Training Period
What is your annual employee turnover percentage? It's a number every Manager and Leader should know because, even if you have a small team of 25 members, constant turnover can be costing your business upwards of $75,000 a year.

If your annual turnover is 100% or higher, that means you started the year with your team of 25 people and, by Christmas, they're all gone, replaced by a new group of people. How costly is that? When recruiting time, materials, orientation and training are tallied, most businesses will spend between $3,000 and $5,000 per person during the first 30 days alone. So if you do the math, it's easy to see why reducing new hire turnover is so critical. But that is just the monetary side of the issue. High turnover also has a significant negative effect on the morale of your existing team.

The 30-30 Rule of Employee Turnover

Many studies suggest that employee turnover occurring within the first 30 days can be reduced by over 30% when:
- Orientation is conducted by the Leader
- A training plan is developed and utilized
- The first full day of training is facilitated by the Leader
- Daily 1-on-1 discussions are held to review progress
- A "pulse check" meeting is conducted after 2 weeks

Ask any employee who has been around for five years or longer why they stay with the company and their answer is often, "Because I feel like the people I work with here are family" or "It's the people. I love working with these folks." As we have learned, the need to belong is one of our greatest human needs.

Creating a sense of belonging to both the organization and the team is what the orientation process <u>should</u> be about. Unfortunately, most orientation programs consist of nothing more than completing some paperwork and watching a video.

As a Leader, it's your challenge to ensure the new hire orientation process is about helping the person fit in and to feel welcome, as though they are a member of the team from day one. If you can accomplish this, the odds that your new hire will remain on the schedule beyond 30 days have just doubled, saving you precious time and money and strengthening your core team, while allowing you to focus more of your time on building the business.

Disposable Team Members

Many Managers treat their team members as though they are disposable. As you will read in the next illustration, I once had a supervisor who clearly had that philosophy and he lived it to the letter. If a member of the team was performing below standard, he did not think of coaching or training the individual – he simply fired them. His Manager mindset was that the best way to upgrade the team is to constantly "turn" the crew. In reality, that resulted in high turnover, business instability, team insecurity and inconsistent operations, all at a staggering financial cost.

You Will Have To Fire Them All
Just out of management training, I was eager for a challenge. My District Manager, Calvin, took me to a few restaurants in his area to meet some of the other Managers. Driving to each location, we traded thoughts concerning our leadership philosophy. He was clearly a champion of the "It's my way or the highway" style of "management". Calvin made it clear that he had little use for all that coaching and team building stuff they teach in training. To him, there was a simple answer to dealing with performance problems. If people would not do things as directed, fire them and hire someone else.

As we pulled into the parking lot of the restaurant that was to be my new assignment, he parked the car, turned off the engine, leaned towards me and said, "Now, Ben, let me give you some history on this restaurant before we go inside. The Manager you are replacing was fired last week. I gave her more chances than I'll give you to turn this restaurant around, so listen up."

Now he really had my attention as he continued. "Sales are down 10% from last year. Transactions are down even more. In terms of cleanliness, this is by far the dirtiest restaurant in my area. We are under threat of closure by the county health department. Customer complaints are high and quality inspection results are the lowest in the entire district. You have 2 assistant managers, 2 shift supervisors and 25 crew members who collectively make up one of the most dysfunctional teams I have ever seen. <u>You will have to fire them all</u>. I expect you to replace the entire team during your first 60 days as General Manager." I sat in stunned silence, not sure of how to respond to his challenge. Firing 29 people was not my idea of good coaching, training or leadership, for that matter.

Opening the car door, Calvin (now grinning and with a sarcastic tone in his voice) said, "I'll bet they didn't teach you *that* in your training class!" But he was wrong. They did teach me how to train, motivate and develop a team. I did learn how to increase sales and transaction counts. What they did not teach me was how to deal with an egotistical, hypocritical, self-centered boss. <u>That</u> I would need to learn on my own. As we entered the restaurant, the words of a respected leader echoed in my head: ==*Never allow the quality of your boss to determine the quality of your work.*== I was determined not to let this person get in the way of my success. Yet, Calvin's 60-day threat was hard to dismiss.

From that first visit, I could see he was not under-selling the condition of the restaurant. This would be a huge challenge. As we left, he asked if I thought I could handle it. Could I turn this place around in 60 days? I remembered the leadership lesson from Coach Johnson and replied with all the confidence I could muster, "Yes, I can!" Secretly, I thought it was mission impossible and I was destined to take my place in the unemployment line. However, I wanted to get in the game and, as both Coach Johnson and my Grandmother had taught me, you must display confidence in your abilities if you expect to be afforded opportunities in life.

Somehow, I had to take this dysfunctional group of people and turn them into a well-oiled machine of a team that would turn the business around.

Observe-Question-Plan-Act

Even as a young Leader, I knew enough about people to realize that walking in with an attitude of "my way or the highway" would be counter-productive. That style would likely cause more problems with the team and I clearly had enough to deal with. Rather than jumping in and making immediate changes, I decided to observe the current operation, ask questions, and get to know the 29 people Calvin had ordered me to fire. During the first 7 days, I took the *Observe-Question-Plan-Act* approach, which caused me to switch hats from "manager" to "leader" quite often. For example:

Manager Thought: *This team has been in place for almost 6 months. They should know their jobs by now, so why aren't they performing? Maybe Calvin was right. I'll need to fire them all.*

Leader Thought: *This team has been in place for almost 6 months. They should know their jobs by now. I wonder why they are making so many mistakes. I'll need to develop them all.*

Manager Thought: *Our inventory is all out of whack due to inaccurate product orders. From now on, I will make out all the product orders to get this under control.*

Leader Thought: *Our inventory is all out of whack due to inaccurate product orders. I'm going to get my leadership team together and retrain them to get the product orders under control.*

Manager Thought: *There is so much to do! I will need to work 7 days a week for the next month.*

Leader Thought: *There is so much to do! I need to get everyone to take as much ownership in this as I have by building their commitment level so I don't have to work 7 days a week.*

Step One: Observe the Operation and Get to Know the Team
When some Managers take on a new assignment, they often will hold a "get to know me" meeting. They use the opportunity to tell the team about themselves, their expectations, their goals. It can be a very "I" centered event. As a Leader, I was more focused on my team than myself, so I took a different approach. I met with the team members one-on-one to learn about them. Remember, Leaders talk less and listen more, so I saw this as my opportunity to do just that. I knew that there would be plenty of time to show the team who I was through my actions. To get to know each team member I asked questions such as:

- Why did you come to work here?
- What do you enjoy most about your work?
- What are your strengths?
- What would you like to improve on?
- What would you like to be doing 3 months from now?

When meeting with my leadership team, I added a few questions:

- What would you like me to know about your leadership style?
- What can I do to help with your professional development?

These questions really got the conversation flowing. And because I did more listening than talking, I was able to learn a lot of relevant information about each team member in a short period of time. After 3 days of one-on-one meetings, I came to the following conclusions:

- The team was very distrustful of leadership because their trust bank account had been drained bone dry by the

previous Manager. I would need to find ways to rebuild trust and credibility.
- The team trained each other on everything. Prior management did not schedule, facilitate or conduct training of any kind. I would need to introduce planned training.
- Most team members had written performance warnings in their personnel file that were not discussed with them or signed by them. From those reports, it appeared as though everyone was an under-performer. Yet I could not see why I would need to fire any of them. They needed a Leader more than a disciplinarian.

Understanding the Origins of Poor Performance
Frustrated Managers who jump into a situation blindly, are tempted to clean house quickly to establish their power base and make a name for themselves (otherwise known as the "I" centered Manager we talked about in Lesson 4). When dealing with performance problems, some Managers actually feel that people make mistakes on purpose, as though it's a conspiracy against them personally. I think they believe the team gathers in the dark of night at some abandoned warehouse to plot how to make the Manager's life miserable. Leaders know better. Very few people make mistakes on purpose. When was the last time that you woke up in the morning, looked in the mirror and said, "I can't wait to get to work today so I can really screw things up?" Instead, most of us wake up each morning, take a deep breath, look in the mirror and say, "I'm going to give it my best today." Understanding this, Leaders know that poor performance is usually due to one of three factors:

1) Lack of knowledge to do the job correctly
2) Ineffective training to do the job efficiently
3) Poor behavior, which is often the result of the person not understanding the "Whys" of their job

Acting as a Manager, we are pretty good at dealing with the first two factors of poor performance. If a person lacks knowledge, the Manager will give them the tools they need to find the knowledge. If a person lacks training, the Manager will provide it and job efficiency will improve. Explaining the "Whys" can be a different matter, and it's what real Leaders do best.

Gain Commitment by Explaining the Real Reason "Why"
When you ask someone to do something in a certain way, there are 3 reasons they should comply with your request.

1) Because it's company policy or a regulation
2) Because you said so (after all, you're the boss)
3) The real reason

Here's an example: One day, I noticed a member of the team standing on a chair to retrieve a box from the top self in the storage area. Obviously, a safety step ladder would be safer to use.
I asked the team member to use the safety ladder, not the chair. The team member asked the obvious question, "Why?" I had 3 choices of how I could respond:

1) It's against company policy to use a chair to stand on.
2) I'm your boss and I'm telling you to use a safety ladder.
3) A lot of people have been seriously injured from falling off chairs. I care about you and don't want you to get hurt!

Managers Demand Compliance – Leaders Build Commitment
Think back to what we learned from the Paco story. We all have a basic human need to be cared about and loved by others. Considering this, which "Why" answer will mean the most to the

BUILDING YOUR TEAM

team member and cause them to change their behavior? "I care about you and don't want you to get hurt!" of course. Company policies can't do that on a personal level. Neither can the intimidation of, "Do it because I'm the boss and I'm telling you to do it." But tell the person you care about their personal safety, they are a valued member of the team and they are needed – that will hit home with just about anyone. And therefore, they will be more likely to do what you ask them to do. Managers say, "Do it because I said so." Leaders teach the "Whys" to people so that they will have a commitment to do the right thing, the right way, for the right reasons, at the right time, whether the boss is watching or not.

There are some folks who manage strictly by compliance, and therefore continue to experience the frustration of inconsistent performance by team members. When I was a multi-unit Leader, one of my General Managers was getting ready to leave for vacation. I said to him, "You must be excited to get some well-deserved time off. I'll bet you are really looking forward to this vacation." He replied, "Actually, I'm dreading this vacation. Things don't run the same when I'm not here. In fact, I just know this place will be all hosed up by the time I get back. I'm not looking forward to that at all!" After some investigating, I discovered that he was a compliance Manager. Everyone did what he said, when he said to do it, and only while he would be watching. But few had any notion as to the real reason why. So whenever he was absent – be it a day off or going on vacation – the team performed below the compliance level because he was not around to check up on them.

Because of this, the Manager actually believed that the restaurant could not operate properly without him, causing him to work 12 hour days and often 6 or 7 days a week.

Step Two: Question Everything

As I observed the team in action, I began asking why things were being done the way they were. Some of the answers were surprising. For example, one morning I discovered a team member "programming" the service timer in a way that made service times appear to be better than they actually were. Why was he doing this? I discovered that my predecessor had threatened the team that if service times did not improve, the work hours of the entire service staff would be cut. Many of the service team members were single-parent wage earners. A reduction in work hours meant a smaller paycheck, which few could afford. Faced with that threat, they did find a way to improve the service times – by manipulating the service timing mechanism! They had no *commitment* to improve service times legitimately. They felt forced to comply.

The Leadership Lesson

Be careful when making demands on performance without understanding the root cause of the performance problem. When people feel pressured to deliver results-on-demand, they may indeed deliver, but *how they do it* may not solve the real problem. In fact, it may cause other problems to develop. In this case, the root problem of the poor service time was three-fold; scheduling, people positioning and cross-training. With these issues addressed, speed of service times legitimately decreased to record lows within 30 days. By determining the root cause of the problem and explaining the "Whys", I was able to gain the team's commitment to resolve the problem. And I was able to accomplish this without the use of intimidation, threats of reduced hours or employment termination.

Step Three: Make a Plan Based on What You Have Learned

After a week of observations and questioning, I had all the information needed to create a specific development plan for both the business and my team. I established a new foundation to build the business for the future. And all of the plans revolved around the training and development of my team, because I knew that without a well-trained team, the plans were meaningless.

Step Four: Put the Plan into Action
During the time I was "questioning everything," I learned that no one, not even my leadership team, was aware of the decline in sales, transactions and profits, let alone the threats of closure coming from the county health department. The big picture had not been presented to them. I could see that my first task was to provide some crystal-clear communication to get everyone on the same page about our situation and their role in the action plans.

Begin With the Leadership Team
My first step was to call a meeting with my leadership team to brief them about the plan for the general team meeting and to review our business action plans. In addition, I assigned a topic to each of them to speak about at the team meeting. All of this came as a surprise to them. In the past, they were never offered to participate in any part of the business other than to run their shifts. Now I had them thinking about the bigger picture of the business and, most importantly, their role in it. I immediately noticed a positive difference in the leadership team's behavior after our meeting.

The following week at the general team meeting, we – the leadership team – presented the facts of our situation and the business plan. By the leadership team presenting a united front, we were in essence saying to the rest of the team "join us" in our effort to turn this situation around. And they did.

The Results
The team began taking ownership in their work, and it showed in every aspect of our operation. By the end of the first 60 days, sales

and transaction counts had gone from -10% to even with the previous year, and building. Service times had steadily improved, (without manipulating the timing mechanism!). Team morale was on the rise. And during a follow-up inspection by the county health department, the inspector stated she had never seen the operation cleaner or the team looking better. We were on our way. And as for Calvin, who had challenged me to "fire them all"; he, too, became a believer. In fact, I had impressed him so much that, after 6 months, I was transferred to – you guessed it – another "challenging" restaurant. It seems that my reward was to do it all over again. Which by the way I did, successfully, using the same process. And years later, as a multi-unit Leader, I utilized the Observe-Question-Plan-Act process and discovered it works at that level as well.

The Leader's Notebook

Key points to remember from Lesson 5:

- Leaders teach the "Whys" to people so they will have a commitment to do the right thing, the right way, for the right reasons, at the right time, whether the boss is watching or not.

- Be careful when making demands on performance without understanding the root cause of the performance problem. When people feel pressured to deliver results-on-demand, they may indeed deliver, but *how they do it* may not solve the real problem.

- Managers Demand Compliance – Leaders Build Commitment.

Recommended Development Actions

Sharpen your leadership skills through these developmental actions:

- To reduce new hire turnover, Leaders should be involved in the initial orientation and training. When you hire a new team member:

  - Participate in the new hire orientation.
  - Participate in their first day of training.
  - Conduct daily 1-on-1 discussions to review progress.
  - Personally conduct a 2 week "pulse check" meeting.

- Know your company's interviewing, hiring and training processes and follow them to the letter.

THE LEADER'S TOOL BOX

As I noted in the beginning of this book, leadership is a journey. Now is the time to start gathering tools that will help you become effective in your new role. When I reflect on my first years of leadership, there were four tools in particular that were very helpful to me, and I believe they will be helpful to you as well:

- A process for creating effective action plans
- A method to prepare your team for the unexpected
- A philosophy for dealing with change
- A template for creating team incentives

T.A.P. (Tactical Action Plan)
Whatever your leadership role may be, resolving problems, improving operations and increasing sales and profits are all part of your responsibility. Creating, leading and executing a "plan" are critical functions for every Leader. Regardless of the planning format you decide to use, know that every effective action plan will contain five key elements that are found in a Tactical Action Plan:

1. The goal is clearly defined
2. Specific tactics are determined
3. Responsibility is assigned
4. Target dates for completion are set
5. A status meeting is scheduled and conducted

Check the following action plan against these five key elements. Would you consider it to be an effective plan?

Restaurant "Z" Action Plan

1. <u>Goal:</u> To increase sales
2. <u>Action Steps:</u> Work to increase the number of catering relationships with the focus on increasing the number of transactions.
3. <u>Person Responsible:</u> Everyone
4. <u>Completion Date:</u> Ongoing
5. <u>Follow Up:</u> Ongoing

This plan lacks the specifics of "who, what and when" that are critical elements to any action plan. Using a Tactical Action Plan format, both success and failure are easy to identify and the lines of accountability are crystal-clear. Here is an example of what a T.A.P. would look like for "Restaurant Z".

<u>5 Steps of the Tactical Action Plan</u>

1) **Define the main objective and specific goal**
   The goal is crystal-clear and easy to measure.

   - Increase sales (main objective)
   5% in March vs. same period last year (specific goal) through increased local catering sales (how)

2) **Determine tactics (actions) to be taken**
   Specific actions that will cause the goal to be accomplished.

   - Create flyer/catering coupon offer

- Hand out 500 flyers w/ coupon offer at trade show
  Contact all local businesses within 5 mile radius with coupon offer – personal visit by staff member
- Conduct follow up sales calls to solicit orders

3) **Assign responsibilities – set target dates**
Determine who is responsible and when it will be completed.

- Create flyer/coupon offer – Margareta – Feb. 18
- Hand out flyers w/ coupon offer at local trade show to each business – Robin and Wendell – Feb. 21
- Visit all local businesses within 5 mile radius with coupon offer – David, Robert, Maria – Feb. 26
- Conduct follow up calls – Maria – Week of March 1

4) **Establish results measurement**
How you will know you are accomplishing the goal.

- Catering report – posted every Monday – David

5) **Schedule status review meetings as needed**
Meet to ensure the plan is on track. Make adjustments.

- Status review meeting: March 12, 1:00pm

Why T.A.P. Works

Tactical Action Plans help you hold people accountable for their responsibilities and recognize those who contribute to solutions, all while keeping your efforts organized and focused to achieve goals. There is also the added benefit of using this process as part of a "to-grow" list. Remember, your responsibility as the Master Gardner of the team is to grow people. Involving your leadership team in the creation and execution of a Tactical Action Plan is one way to do just that.

Prepare For the Unexpected
Stuff Happens. I call them the SH events. Sometimes we see them coming and sometimes they seem to come out of nowhere. I have found that Managers and Leaders have different approaches in dealing with SH events. Managers will do what they do best. Wait for something to happen and then "manage" through the event. Leaders, on the other hand, will <u>anticipate</u> SH events and be ready with a "Plan B". Half the battle of successfully dealing with the unexpected is having a plan for how to respond – if and when – stuff happens. The other half is execution – making the right moves at the right time. As a Leader, it's our job to help prepare our teams for the SH factors that may occur. Hosting regular team meetings to review your company's policies and procedures can be helpful. Conducting quick one-on-one discussions can also be effective. But I'd like to offer the following as a fun, engaging method of preparing the team for the SH events that are sure to come your way sooner or later.

Let's Play "What If"
I prepared my leadership teams for the SH events by playing the "What If" game. For example, during a visit I would ask questions such as: "What if 2 employees called in sick right now. How would you cover their shifts?" or "What if the POS system crashed right now? How would you manage the business?" or "Suppose a customer reports a tornado on the ground and it's moving this way. What are the first three things you would do to protect your team and customers?" After getting initial responses, I would suggest we look up the answer in the company manual. This part of the exercise reinforces not only <u>how</u> to get the answer, but <u>where</u> to get the answer as well. I was always amazed at the number of conflicting

responses I would receive; an indication that, as a team, we were not all on the same page.

When you are talking about urgent or emergency situations, it is critical that everyone on the team knows exactly what to do. Having 5 different views on how to respond to an emergency can result in confusion during a time when every second counts. My "What If" session would end with the participants reviewing both the question and the answer back to me to be sure we were all on the same page. The entire process takes less than 10 minutes per topic. I typically would introduce one new topic each week. As you can imagine, through the years my teams experienced their fair share of "What Ifs" – everything from power failures and medical emergencies to armed robberies. I'm proud to say that my teams were always well prepared, knowing exactly how to respond in these situations, due in large part to our weekly "What If" games.

Dealing with Change – A Leader's Perspective
I read a news article that seemed to describe the ever-changing world we live in. Here is a portion of that article:

"This world is too big for us. There is too much going on, too many crimes, casualties, and violence. Try as you will, you get behind in spite of yourself. It is an incessant strain to keep pace and still you lose ground. Science empties its discoveries on you so fast that you stagger beneath them in hopeless bewilderment. The political world witnesses new scenes so rapidly that you can get out of breath just trying to keep up. Everything is high-pressure. I don't think human nature can endure much more."

When I first read this, I felt it reflected how many people must feel about change in today's world. I was surprised to discover that this article was actually published in the *Atlantic Journal* in the year 1837! It seems that, even then, during a time most people today consider to be the good old days of a slower paced society, change was tough to deal with. But here's the good news: As much as change can be bewildering, overwhelming and even frightening, there are actually some things that don't change. They are what many people consider to be the intangibles of life. The best example of this is reflected in an open letter to school children that was written by the author of the <u>Little House on the Prairie</u> books, Laura Ingalls Wilder. Ms. Wilder was a school teacher from 1882–1885 before writing the "Little House" books. She was asked how schools of the present day (in 1956) had changed compared to the schools she attended over 70 years ago. This was her response:

"The <u>Little House</u> books that I wrote are stories of long ago. The way we live and our schools are much different now. So many changes have made living and learning much easier. But the <u>real</u> things haven't changed. It is still best to be honest and truthful, to make the most of what we have, to be happy with simple pleasures, to be cheerful, and to have courage when things go wrong."

As Leaders, we can help our teams get through times of change by keeping them focused on the things that really matter. Compare each of these views on the topic of change. Leadership is a choice. As a Leader, which view will you choose to champion?

Change Is Scary
Despite the fact that most people recognize change as a necessary part of life, most of us dread it. We understand that, for better or worse, nothing stays the same forever. Yet the uncertainty of change – brought on by all the "what if" questions that develop – can cause our anxiety level to spike to new heights. It is this uncertainty of what the future holds that tears at us. So the question is, how do we find a delicate balance of facing our fear of the unknown with the knowledge that everything must (and will) change? Here's what I know: As Leaders, we can ease the anxiety brought

on by change if we reduce the fear of the unknown. The most powerful tool we have at our disposal to do this is communication. The more information people have, the more comfortable they will be when a change occurs.

The Leadership Lesson
When implementing a change, no matter how large or small, communication is key. Keep the team "in-the-know" of pending changes. Give them time to warm up to the change and to get their questions answered. Reduce their anxiety level through the use of crystal-clear communications.

Individual Incentives vs. Team Incentives
Sitting in a cubical at the car dealership, I was excited to sign the papers on my new car. While waiting, I noticed posters on the wall announcing a sales contest. The salesperson with the highest number of new car sales for the month would win a trip to Orlando, Florida for two. I said to my salesperson, "You must be pretty excited about this contest. How are you doing so far?"
Her reply surprised me. "Oh, I gave up trying weeks ago. There's no way I can win."

That comment caused me to think about my restaurant Leaders. Just the day before, I had announced an area contest with my 9 General Manager Leaders. The restaurant with the highest average check increase would be awarded $200 for a team pizza party. My intent was to "motivate" the Leaders who would, in turn, "inspire" their teams to suggest additional items with meal orders. In the restaurant business, increasing the average check causes other things to increase, including sales, profit margins and staff productivity. After hearing the salesperson's comment, I wondered if my Leaders were saying the same thing – they knew they could not win, so why even try?

A New Approach
The next day, I contacted Amy, a General Manager Leader who was on my "to-grow" list, and asked for her advice. Amy gave it to me straight. "Actually, Ben, we all know Winston has the best team in the area and he will win the contest." She did not need to finish her statement, because I knew what would come next "….so the rest of us figured there is no point in trying." It was time for a new approach. With Amy's help, I changed the contest. We set an area goal for the average check increase. All 9 restaurants would work as one entity towards the goal, each making their own specific contribution to the total team effort. We would all win (or lose) together. And it worked! Not only did we achieve the goal, but we exceeded it by 12 points, receiving national recognition from the organization for our results. Since everyone was a winner, I had to plan 3 pizza parties! But in the end, the additional planning and cost was more than worth it. The contest was a success, my leadership team came together as never before and we exceed the profit margin goal set for the area. <u>Everyone</u> was a winner.

The Leadership Lesson
We all like to win and to be on a winning team. Leaders can build on this desire by structuring incentives in a way that provides everyone equal opportunity to win, as part of a team.

A LEADERSHIP ACORN

Many years ago, my parents lived in a house that was located on a heavily wooded lot filled with huge oak trees. Although beautiful, they often produced thousands of acorns that would litter the driveway and garage. One afternoon, while visiting with my wife and daughters, my stepfather asked if I would sweep out the garage, as the acorns were beginning to pile up. So I began the task of sweeping up acorns and dumping them into an old trash barrel.

I was about half-way through the job, when all of a sudden I heard my 7 year old daughter, Cara, scream in her highest high-pitched voice: *"Daddy!"* It was one of those screams that will catch a parent's attention – if you are a parent, you know the sound. I stopped sweeping and turned around to find her staring at me with the most astonished look on her face. Startled, I asked, "What…what's wrong?" Cara stared back, eyes glaring. It was clear that I was in big trouble. "*What* are you doing?" she shouted. "Nothing," I replied, "Just sweeping up these acorns." "But, Daddy, you're throwing them away!" Now I was confused. "So?" I asked, as I continued sweeping. Then my young daughter gave me a Lesson in Leadership. She said:

"In school I learned that if you plant acorns in the ground and water them, they will grow into trees. Throwing away an acorn is like throwing away a tree. Let's plant one, water it and watch it grow."

In some respects, this book is your Leadership Acorn. You have a choice of what you can do with it. You can toss it away or you can use it to plant some ideas. Ideas that, when nurtured, will enhance your skills and guide you in your journey to become the great coach and Leader you want to be.

It is my hope that you will chose to plant this acorn and begin your move from Manager to Leader. Good luck!

WORDS OF WISDOM

About Leadership
Leadership is a privilege. The people that truly believe this are the most effective Leaders, mentors, coaches and managers. *Aylwin Lewis*

What Leaders Do When Things Go Wrong
Leaders don't point a finger – they lend a hand. *Ben Olson*

True Success
The true measure of success lies not so much in what you have achieved, but in whether you have made a difference. It's knowing you have touched the lives of others, and have in some way made the world a little bit brighter, a little bit better. *Anonymous*

Choices We Make
The events in our lives may shape us, but it's the choices we make that define us. *Tony Robbins*

People Who Constantly Disappoint You
When people show you who they are, believe them. *Maya Angelou*

Follow Your Heart
Follow your heart but take your brain with you. *Zig Ziglar*

Get Back Up
The greatest glory in living lies not in never falling, but in rising every time we fall. *Nelson Mandela*

Leaders Take the Initiative
If it's going to be, it's up to me. *Robert H. Schuller*

First Steps
Don't get discouraged during the first steps of a tough project. Building the basement is always dirty work. *Aylwin Lewis*

Achievement
Getting something done is an accomplishment; getting something done <u>right</u> is an achievement. *Unknown*

Crystal-Clear Communication
If you want everyone to be on the same page, you have to show them the page. *Pam Boyd*

Leadership by Example
You can't <u>make</u> people do anything. The most you can hope for is to show them how to do it, and then say, follow me. *Isaac Stern*

Teaching the Whys
Leaders teach the "Whys" to people so that they will have a commitment to do the right thing, the right way, for the right reasons, at the right time, whether the boss is watching or not. *Ben Olson*

Credibility
Just because you have lost your way doesn't mean your compass is broken. *Anonymous*

Integrity
What lies behind us and what lies before us are small matters compared to what lies within us. *R. W. Emerson*

Dealing with Change
When the winds of change blow, some build walls while others build windmills. *Chinese Proverb*

Attitude
The only true disability in life is a bad attitude. *Scott Hamilton*

About Serving Others
We make a living by what we get; we make a life by what we give. *Duane Hulse*

Communication
The first duty of love is to listen. *Paul Tillich*

Move On With Your Life
You can't start the next chapter of your life if you keep re-reading the last one. Turn the page. *Zig Ziglar*

RECOMMENDED RESOURCES

I hope that reading <u>Lessons in Leadership</u> has inspired you to learn more about becoming a great Leader. There are several wonderful books available that will help you to continue your learning excursion. Here are some of my favorites:

The World's Most Powerful Leadership Principle
How to Become a Servant Leader
James C. Hunter

Leadership 101
What Every Leader Needs to Know
John C. Maxwell

You Don't Need a Title to Be a Leader
Mark Sanborn

Lincoln on Leadership
Executive Strategies for Tough Times
Donald T. Phillips

Soar With Your Strengths
Donald O. Clifton and Paula Nelson

In addition to these books, I highly recommend aspiring Leaders to attend a leadership seminar or workshop once a year. Having the opportunity to network with others is simply priceless. Here are three organizations that offer outstanding leadership workshops:

The American Society of Training and Development (ASTD)
ASTD Leadership Development
www.astd.org

Ken Blanchard
Leadership Training and Development
www.kenblanchard.com

SkillPath Seminars
The Conference on Leadership Development and Teambuilding
www.skillpath.com

ABOUT THE AUTHOR

As a Learning Tour Guide with over 30 years of food service, retail management and training experience, Ben Olson has experienced leadership from the perspective of both the Leader and the follower. His keen observations of leadership behavior both in and out of the business world have made him a sought after speaker, mentor and coach.

Certified as a Master Trainer by The American Society of Training and Development and founder of Customized Performance Training, Ben works as a training consultant designing and delivering his special Brand of training to companies large and small across the country. His first book, Great Trainers Make it Happen! was published in 2007.

Ben is an active member of a variety of organizations, including the American Society of Training and Development (ASTD) and the National Environmental Health Association. He is also a licensed instructor with the National Registry of Food Safety Professionals, National Restaurant Association Educational Foundation and the Illinois Department of Public Health.

You can visit Ben's website at www.CPtrainer.net or send an email with your comments about Lessons in Leadership to:
Ben.Olson@CPtrainer.net

Made in the USA
San Bernardino, CA
06 June 2014